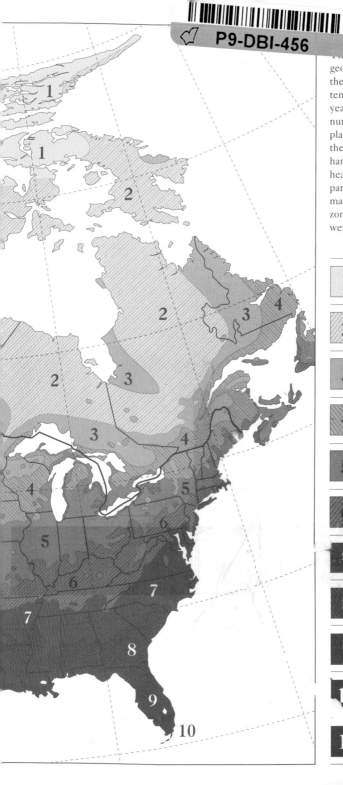

This map shows eleven geographical zones based on the average annual minimum temperatures recorded for the years 1974 to 1986. The zone numbers accompanying the plants in this book indicate their lower limits of winter cold hardiness. Extreme summer heat and humidity also play a part in a plant's adaptability; many plants hardy in colder zones grow poorly in warmer, wetter ones.

1	BELOW −50°F BELOW −46°C
2	−50° TO −40°F −46° TO −40°C
3	−40° TO −30°F −40° TO −34°C
4	−30° TO −20°F −34° TO −29°C
5	−20° TO −10°F −29° TO −23°C
6	−10° TO 0°F −23° TO −18°C
7	0° TO 10°F −18° TO −12°C
8	10° TO 20°F −12° TO −7°C
9	20° TO 30°F −7° TO −1°C
10	30° TO 40°F −1° TO 4°C
11	ABOVE 40°F ABOVE 4°C

P9-DBI-456

EYEWITNESS
GARDEN
HANDBOOKS
PRUNING
&TRAINING

EYEWITNESS

GARDEN
HANDBOOKS

PRUNING
&TRAINING

A DK PUBLISHING BOOK
www.dk.com

635.04

A DK PUBLISHING BOOK
www.dk.com

EDITORIAL CONSULTANT Lin Hawthorne

PROJECT EDITOR Jennifer Jones

ART EDITOR Ursula Dawson

US EDITOR Mary Sutherland

DTP DESIGNER Matthew Greenfield

MANAGING EDITOR Mary-Clare Jerram

MANAGING ART EDITOR Lee Griffiths

PRODUCTION Ruth Charlton

First American Edition, 1999

2 4 6 8 10 9 7 5 3 1

Published in the United States by
DK Publishing, Inc.
95 Madison Avenue
New York, New York 10016

Copyright © 1999
Dorling Kindersley Limited, London

Published in Great Britain by Dorling Kindersley Limited

Library of Congress Cataloging-in-Publication Data

Pruning and training
p. cm. - (Eyewitness garden handbooks)
Includes index.
ISBN 0-7894-4148-9 (alk. paper)
1. Pruning - Handbooks, manuals, etc.
2. Plants - Training - Handbooks, manuals, etc. I. Title. II. Series.
SB125 .B754 1999   635'.044 - dc21   98-32292 CIP

Reproduction by Colourscan, Singapore
Printed and bound in Singapore by Star Standards Industries (Pte) Ltd.

CONTENTS

INTRODUCTION

AT THE SIMPLEST LEVEL, pruning and training aims
to make sure that plants are as healthy and
vigorous as possible, free of structural weakness,
and at the least risk of being infected with disease.
With additional knowledge of how pruning and
training affects the way that plants grow, the
gardener can not only improve their natural
appearance but also enhance their ornamental
value, create striking plant features, or increase
crop yield and quality. Understanding the
principles of a plant's response to pruning is
absolutely key to realizing its full potential, but
you should always bear in mind that, at any stage
in its life, pruning causes some stress to a plant. It
should never be done without good reason or
without a clear idea in your mind of the intended
effects of each and every pruning cut you make.

Trained clematis   *A twining climber, clematis eagerly scrambles up and over a rustic tripod.*

How Plants Grow

THROUGH PRUNING AND training, a gardener can influence the ways in which a plant develops and performs; to do this effectively, it is essential to have a basic understanding of how plants grow in the wild.

PLANT GROWTH

For plants to grow, they must have air, water, nutrients, and light. Growth in height, or extension growth, is made by rapidly dividing cells behind the topmost (apical) bud. The apical bud imposes "apical dominance," producing hormones that move down the stem and inhibit growth of the side buds. These develop only when the leading shoot has been damaged or removed by pruning, or has grown away strongly. If this occurs, a lower sideshoot may reimpose apical dominance.

Parts of a plant
Cellular activity is most active at soft, green shoot tips, where hormones stimulate and control the plant's growth.

Apical or terminal bud ("growing point")

Leading shoot ("leader")

Sublateral, or sideshoot, develops from a bud on a lateral

Axillary buds form in the leaf axils

Apical or terminal bud of lateral shoot

A lateral shoot arises from a side bud (lateral, or axillary, bud)

Stems thicken and become woody as they age

Leaves and shoots develop from a point known as a node; the stem between nodes is an internode

Roots thicken with age to form strong anchorage and may act as a food store

Fibrous feeder roots absorb water and nutrients from the soil through fine root hairs

BUD ARRANGEMENT

Alternate buds arise singly at intervals on alternate sides of a plant's stem. Opposite buds occur in pairs at the same node.

ALTERNATE BUDS   OPPOSITE BUDS

INCREASING GIRTH

Another area of intense cellular activity is in the cambium layer, a band of cells that surrounds the stem just beneath the bark. As cambium cells divide and diversify, stem girth increases. They also form vascular bundles, which run the length of the stems, carrying water and soil nutrients to the leaves, and carbohydrates and plant hormones down the stem to the rest of the plant.

GAINING STRENGTH

Robust stems are formed by a process known as lignification ("becoming woody"), in which specialized strengthening tissue develops. It is stimulated by stem movement, such as that caused by flexing in the wind. This is why low stakes, or no stakes at all, are preferable during a tree's early years – this allows stem flexing and helps to produce strong trunks.

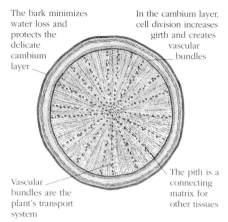

The bark minimizes water loss and protects the delicate cambium layer

In the cambium layer, cell division increases girth and creates vascular bundles

Vascular bundles are the plant's transport system

The pith is a connecting matrix for other tissues

Cross section through a plant stem
Targeted cell activity in the stem insures that it gains bulk and becomes strong, while carrying nourishment throughout the plant.

PHOTOSYNTHESIS

Plants manufacture energy by photosynthesis, a process that occurs mainly in the leaves. A green pigment, chlorophyll, traps the sun's energy, using it to convert carbon dioxide and water into sugars and starch, the food source of the plant. During pruning, the plant is deprived of leafy top growth; the more of this material you remove, and the more frequently you prune, the greater the plant's demand for water and nutrients to fuel new growth. To insure healthy regrowth, apply a balanced fertilizer after pruning.

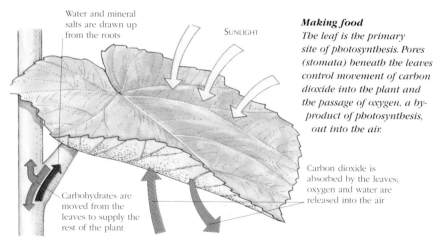

Water and mineral salts are drawn up from the roots

SUNLIGHT

Carbohydrates are moved from the leaves to supply the rest of the plant

Making food
The leaf is the primary site of photosynthesis. Pores (stomata) beneath the leaves control movement of carbon dioxide into the plant and the passage of oxygen, a by-product of photosynthesis, out into the air.

Carbon dioxide is absorbed by the leaves; oxygen and water are released into the air

HOW PLANT GROWTH ADAPTS

The aim of plants is to grow to maturity so they can reproduce, usually by seed. Plants grow toward sunlight, branching to expose maximum leaf area to the sun to optimize photosynthesis; they extend their roots for anchorage and to exploit the soil for moisture and nutrients. Woody plants develop bark that is cold- and weather-resistant in order to survive from year to year and so maximize their potential for reproduction. Top growth, the site of photosynthesis, may be killed in harsh weather, and deciduous woody plants avoid this by dropping their leaves, to become dormant in winter. Plants can survive periods of cold, drought, and other adversities by regenerating from dormant buds on their tough, woody tissue. This ability, inherent in all woody plants to a greater or lesser degree, is the key to how a plant responds to pruning.

Dead wood is isolated by a natural barrier

Stem dieback (left)
A stub left by incorrect pruning dies back, but a natural barrier halts the dieback, permitting new growth from healthy dormant buds.

Cut straight across the line between live and dead wood

Renewal growth (right)
New growth from dormant buds at the base of this rose insures survival if the main stems succumb to damage or disease, or die of old age.

LIFE-THREATENING DAMAGE

As a tree matures, its girth increases and branches develop to expose the maximum leaf area to the sun. If all goes well, a tree naturally forms structurally strong branches. Sometimes, however, a young branch arises at a narrow angle to the trunk, creating a crotch that is inherently weak. As the branch gains weight and mass, the forces on the narrow crotch are such that it can be split in a strong wind. If the damage has occurred at a large branch crotch on a single-trunked tree, neither tree nor gardener may be able to remedy it, and professional advice must be sought. It may be necessary to fell the tree. By removing shoots likely to develop into such branches through correct pruning and training in the early years, such damage could have been prevented in later life.

Split-branch crotch
Wind has split this narrow-angled branch from the trunk, causing life-threatening damage. Corrective early pruning would prevent such branches from developing.

SURVIVING DAMAGE AND DISEASE

Many plants are able to limit the spread of disease, which can gain access through soft or damaged tissue. In response to infection, a plant produces chemicals that form a natural barrier across the stem, thus isolating the diseased portion from the main body of the plant. Woody plants respond to wounding in a similar way, by transporting protective chemicals to the wound site to isolate the damaged tissue and prevent the entry of disease. Scar tissue, or "callus," grows over the wound to form an air- and watertight seal. When making pruning cuts, the aim should always be to reinforce the plant's own natural defenses. Make cuts as small and clean as possible, at a point where the plant's defenses are most active, at a node on the stem or just beyond the branch collar, which is a slight swelling at the base of a branch where it meets the main trunk.

CROSS SECTION THROUGH A BRANCH CROTCH

The bark ridge, where branch and trunk meet

Best place to cut

Branch collar

Cutting branches
Always cut just beyond the branch collar, at an equal and opposite angle to the bark ridge. Never cut into the bark ridge.

Target pruning
A small, clean cut was made just beyond the branch collar. Scar tissue, or callus, closes over the wound rapidly and keeps the plant's natural defense barriers intact.

BREAKING APICAL DOMINANCE

Hormones produced by the leading bud flow down the stem to inhibit the growth of laterals, or sideshoots. With the terminal bud intact (*right*), apical dominance is maintained, and vigor is directed primarily into further upward growth. When the terminal bud is removed (*far right*), the flow of these hormones is reduced. The topmost remaining bud then grows more strongly, but does not have absolute dominance, and the buds lower down begin branching out. This universal principle is at the basis of many pruning cuts that promote branching, whether pinching out growing tips from soft stems or removing the leading shoots on trees or shrubs.

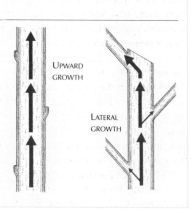

UPWARD GROWTH

LATERAL GROWTH

HOW PRUNING WORKS

THE KEY FACT UNDERLYING all pruning and training techniques is that when material is removed from a plant or a stem is tied down horizontally, the plant will usually respond by making new growth elsewhere. Gardeners can prune to induce growth where and when it is wanted, and thus vary the direction, quantity, and vigor of this growth as desired.

RESPONSES TO PRUNING

Many plants will respond well to a variety of pruning techniques, but it is very important, when choosing plants for special treatment, to be sure that they will react in the desired way. It is not safe to assume that all plants in the same genus respond in the same way to pruning. They often do, but they may equally well vary widely in their growth habit and flowering season, two major factors to be taken into account when choosing suitable pruning techniques. Plants within a genus may also vary in their tolerance of pruning, so while one is stimulated by hard pruning, another may die of shock.

One species, two effects
Syringa meyeri *is naturally neat and bushy* (above), *with branches down to the ground, but it responds well to training as a clear-stemmed standard* (left).

THE GROWING TIP

Removing the terminal (apical) bud on a leading shoot breaks its apical dominance *(see p.11)*. Side buds lower down on the stem, often latent in leaf axils, are stimulated into activity and develop into shoots. If these in turn have their tips pinched out, and so on, the effect is a proliferation of growth. This is key both to creating dense, bushy growth and inducing new shoots that will grow, or can be trained, in the desired direction. Pinch-pruning *(see pp.66–7)* uses this technique to great effect.

Pruning for bushy growth
This coleus shows clearly the effect of removing a terminal bud. A single-stemmed plant will branch freely if all its shoot tips are pinched out.

BEFORE   AFTER

SAME GENUS, DIFFERENT HABIT

Botanical classification groups plants into a genus according to shared characteristics, like flower form and petal number. A genus includes a number of species, and within species there may be "cultivars" with their own distinct characteristics. The very different plants shown are both honeysuckles. *Lonicera japonica* is climbing, while *L. nitida* 'Baggesen's Gold' is shrubby. Since pruning needs depend on habit and flowering time, the requirements of species within a genus may vary considerably.

LONICERA NITIDA 'BAGGESEN'S GOLD'

LONICERA JAPONICA

HORIZONTAL TRAINING

Pulling a vertical stem down and tying it in horizontally has similar effects to removing the leading, or terminal, shoot (*see p.11 and opposite, below*). It reduces the sap flow so that the terminal bud loses much of its dominance. Instead of relentlessly pursuing upward growth, the stem diverts its energy into producing a number of sideshoots simultaneously from buds along its length; all will grow upward with similar vigor and are much more likely to produce a good show of flowers and fruits. This technique is ideal for climbing and other long, flexible-stemmed plants grown directly up or along flat surfaces such as walls and fences, giving maximum coverage and an even distribution of flowers. It is also the principle behind cordon or espaliered fruit trees, where decorative forms are combined with increased yields.

MAXIMIZING FLOWERING AND FRUITING

Vertical stem
The natural tendency of this rose's unpruned main shoot and its sideshoot is to grow upward toward sunlight. This means that a tall, leggy plant develops, with flowers produced only at the top of the stems and possibly out of sight.

Upward growth

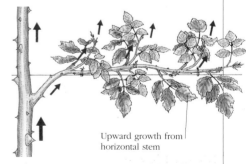

Upward growth from horizontal stem

Horizontal stem
Tying a shoot down allows sideshoots to grow out from buds in the leaf axils; these nearly always flower and fruit more freely.

WHY PRUNE?

BEFORE YOU MAKE A SINGLE CUT, there are two vital points to consider: first, always assess the whole plant, and second, never prune without good reason. There are, however, many good reasons to prune, which include removing dead, diseased, or damaged wood to insure continued good health, improving flowering, or shaping young plants to a desired form.

MAINTAINING FORM AND EFFECT

One reason for pruning is to guarantee a well-shaped specimen that is strong and healthy and which displays its desirable features to best effect. Most trees, for example, grow naturally with a single leader and an evenly distributed framework of branches above a clear trunk. Many need little, if any, pruning to produce this desirable form, but sometimes trees will produce two leaders –

a situation that must be remedied if the tree is to be structurally sound at maturity. Many ornamentals are grown for desirable features such as attractively variegated foliage. If they revert, that is produce all-green leaves, pruning is needed to preserve the decorative qualities for which they were chosen.

Dual leaders (right)
If a leading shoot is damaged, a tree may produce dual leaders that form a narrow-angled crotch. At maturity, the branches may break away from the trunk (see p.10). The situation should be remedied as soon as possible by removing the weaker leader.

A well-formed specimen tree
Nyssa sylvatica *is grown as a central-leader standard; the lower branches have been cleared from the trunk to display the typical "starburst" habit to beautiful effect.*

Cutting out reversion
If not removed as soon as they occur, all-green shoots out-compete their variegated counterparts; they contain more chlorophyll and so are nearly always more vigorous.

SHAPING GROWTH

Pruning to shape growth can be as simple as cutting back to a bud that faces in the desired direction, but sometimes growth becomes unbalanced and more positive action is needed. In this case, it is essential to understand how pruning affects the vigor of regrowth. In general, the harder the pruning, the more vigorous the regrowth. Conversely, pruning lightly, or not at all, results in limited regrowth.

CORRECTING UNEVEN GROWTH

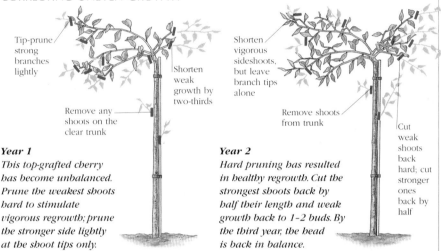

Tip-prune strong branches lightly

Remove any shoots on the clear trunk

Shorten weak growth by two-thirds

Shorten vigorous sideshoots, but leave branch tips alone

Remove shoots from trunk

Cut weak shoots back hard; cut stronger ones back by half

Year 1
This top-grafted cherry has become unbalanced. Prune the weakest shoots hard to stimulate vigorous regrowth; prune the stronger side lightly at the shoot tips only.

Year 2
Hard pruning has resulted in healthy regrowth. Cut the strongest shoots back by half their length and weak growth back to 1–2 buds. By the third year, the head is back in balance.

REMOVING SUCKERS

Suckers from roots or epicormic shoots on stems occur spontaneously or in response to damage. Suckers can be a nuisance by spreading beyond their allotted space. Cut them off at their point of origin, and pare the surrounding tissue with a knife to take off any dormant buds nearby. New buds often grow around wounds made by removing epicormic shoots. They are best rubbed out before they grow, but otherwise, remove as soon as seen.

Suckers (left)
Willows are especially prone to producing root suckers; they seldom harm the tree but may intrude where they are not wanted.

Epicormic shoots (right)
These arise from dormant buds on the trunk, often as an unwanted response to pruning. If not removed, they are likely to proliferate, taking energy from the tree.

Cut off at the point of origin

15

PRUNING FOR HEALTH

For many plants, pruning needs are very simple, since they require little other than the removal of dead, diseased, or damaged shoots to keep them in good health. Plants are often able to limit the spread of disease by forming natural barriers that isolate damaged tissue (*see pp.10–11*). The aim of pruning out damaged tissue is to help the plant recover full health without breaching the natural barriers. Dead wood is removed because it can harbor infection. If a plant has already formed a natural barrier between live and dead wood, the general rule is not to cut below it, or the plant will have to expend energy needlessly by forming either scar tissue or another barrier farther down the stem. In some cases, however, it is necessary to cut back into live, healthy wood. Some exceptions to the general rule are outlined here.

Frost damage
Cut back frost damage to live wood, but not when more frost is likely. Such cuts will expose new buds to further frost damage.

Snow-damaged santolina
Prune santolina back hard in early spring into old wood to stimulate new, bushy evergreen growth from the base.

Torn bark and jagged wounds may allow wood-rotting diseases to enter

Damaged branch
If a new branch at this point is desired, cut straight across below all damage, to a node, if visible. Do not breach the branch collar.

REMOVING DAMAGE

Branches that are partially broken, for example by lightning damage, the weight of snow, or the action of vandals or grazing animals, are best dealt with quickly because torn branches and bark often leave large wounds that can be colonized rapidly by wood-rotting pathogens. These damaged branches rarely mend if tied back in position. It is usually better to remove the branch (*see p.23*), or shorten it to a suitable replacement shoot below the damage. If shoots fail to develop in the following growing season, remove the stub.

FEEDING AND MULCHING

While removal of dead, diseased, or damaged wood is always positively beneficial to the plant, other types of pruning inevitably remove healthy material in active growth. Removing leafy growth for purely ornamental reasons deprives the plant of energy-producing material (*see p. 9*), while stimulating abundant flowering or fruiting makes considerable demands on the plant. If a plant is to remain healthy and not be unduly stressed by pruning, it must have water and nutrients to fuel new growth.

- Use a complete fertilizer containing a balanced formulation of nitrogen, potassium, and phosphates, with essential trace elements.
- In spring, apply a balanced fertilizer to the base of the plant, using the recommended rate. Make sure the soil is damp first. If

repeated applications are needed, do not apply after midsummer; late soft growth is vulnerable to cold damage.

- Apply a mulch of organic matter (*see below*), 3–4in (8–10cm) deep, to conserve moisture and reduce weed competition. Do not allow the mulch to touch the stem.

MUSHROOM COMPOST   WELL-ROTTED MANURE

DEAD WOOD

When woody tissue becomes diseased, the tree or shrub responds by forming a natural chemical barrier to isolate the problem. In most cases, provided the disease is not too widespread, the infected part – deprived of nourishment by the barrier – eventually dies and is shed. If left in place, unshed dead wood provides a host for fungal rots as it decays, posing a health hazard to the tree.

The junction between dead and living tissue is often distinctly marked (*see p. 10*) and this is the point at which dead wood is best removed. If the disease is still active, however, there may be no clear demarcation line. After making the cut, inspect the cut surface carefully. If disease or discoloration is still visible, more wood must be cut away.

Canker

Healthy tissue

Diseased wood
The branch shown here is infected with canker, a fungal disease that rapidly invades living tissue. The main stem is discolored and dying back, but there is no clear demarcation line between healthy and diseased tissue. The affected growth is cut back to clean living tissue that shows no sign of infection. A small, neat cut made with clean sharp pruners will heal rapidly.

Dead patches in conifers
Remove dead material and disguise the resulting hole by tying adjacent branches to a cane inserted at the center of the gap.

ORNAMENTAL EFFECTS

Several techniques can be used to enhance a plant's ornamental virtues. In some cases, trees with beautiful bark – particularly the birches – can be pruned to create multi-stemmed specimens, thus maximizing their most attractive feature. But the most obvious example is pruning to increase flower and berry production, which is often combined with training to a specific form to enhance a plant's decorative potential.

Pruning for flowering
Unpruned stems of Chaenomeles (left) *produce few flowers. Cutting sideshoots back to 2–3 buds creates free-flowering spurs* (right).

Multistemmed trees
Betula nigra *often takes a multistemmed form. Most birches can be made to do this by cutting back close to the ground in their early years.*

ANNUAL RENEWAL

Most shrubs flower more freely on young wood, either directly from new shoots, as with most buddleias, or on lateral growth that arises from old wood. Ensuring the continuous production of fresh new shoots is key to consistent flowering. Annual removal in late winter or early spring of some of the oldest growth induces new shoots and allows light to reach the center of the plant so that the wood can ripen.

Remove old, badly placed growth

Cut back last year's stems to 2–3 pairs of buds

Deciduous shrub flowering on young wood
Buddleja davidii *flowers on the current year's growth in summer. Cutting back hard induces strong straight flowering stems. Left unpruned, buddlejas may become leggy and tangled.*

PRODUCTIVE TRAINING

Growing plants against a wall or other support not only displays them to advantage but may also improve the productivity of the plant. In most species, training stems horizontally breaks the apical dominance of leading shoots, causing them to produce laterals (*see p.13*). In many plants, especially those in the rose family, the laterals produce significantly more flowers and fruit. This is the main reason why apples and pears are sometimes grown as cordons or espaliers. With a wall-trained pyracantha, the berries are revealed in all their glory by additional pruning in late summer to remove young shoots that would otherwise mask the ripening fruits.

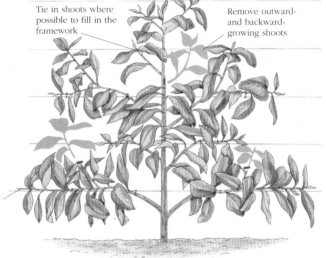

Wall-trained tree
Training Magnolia grandiflora *against a wall helps protect it from cold and aids good ripening of wood by summer sun. Well-ripened wood always flowers more.*

Tie in shoots where possible to fill in the framework

Remove outward- and backward-growing shoots

When branches fill the allotted space, pinch out their shoot tips to induce growth of flowering laterals

Wall-trained shrub
The arching main stems of pyracantha lend themselves well to horizontal training, producing a higher percentage of flowers and fruits as a result.

SHRUBS FOR WALLS

BUDDLEJA CRISPA,
  B. FALLOWIANA
CEANOTHUS (evergreen)
CHAENOMELES
CHIMONANTHUS PRAECOX
COTONEASTER HORIZONTALIS
CYTISUS BATTANDIERI
FREMONTODENDRON
FUCHSIA ARBORESCENS
MAGNOLIA GRANDIFLORA
PIPTANTHUS NEPALENSIS
PRUNUS MUME,
  P. TRILOBA 'MULTIPLEX'
PYRACANTHA
RIBES SANGUINEUM,
  R. SPECIOSUM

SPECIAL EFFECTS

Several pruning techniques can be used - in conjunction with training - for purely ornamental purposes. Topiary has long been used in formal gardens to create strongly architectural and geometric shapes. The same skills and principles used to create the complex and whimsical forms, like peacocks and chess pieces for large gardens, can be used to train eyecatching features for small spaces. Cones, obelisks, and columns are relatively easy to produce, since they require no intricate training and can usually be created from single young specimens (*see pp. 52-3*).

Topiary forms
A clear-stemmed standard (left) *or elegant spiral* (right) *in a container makes a perfect centerpiece for a courtyard; a pair can line a path or flank a doorway.*

PINCH-PRUNED SHAPES

Similar - though more short-term - "topiary" effects can be created relatively quickly by pinch-pruning (*see pp. 66–7*) rapidly growing evergreen subshrubs such as *Santolina* or, as shown here, *Helichrysum petiolare*. These subshrubs, which produce soft, annual top- growth on a permanent woody base, give attractive results in one or two growing seasons. Once the desired shape has been reached, with careful cultivation it can last for several years. Here, three single-stemmed young plants share a 9in (23cm) pot. They are first trained upward on a cane "wigwam"; then, using the canes as a guide, all of the shoot tips are pinched out each week to form the shape and induce dense bushy growth. The finished cone may reach a height of 4–5ft (1.2–1.5m).

Helichrysum cone
This pinch-pruned helichrysum makes an unusual focal-point for a patio or courtyard during summer. In cold climates, bring it in for the winter for indoor decoration.

FOR FOLIAGE EFFECTS

ACER NEGUNDO,
  A. NEGUNDO 'FLAMINGO'
AILANTHUS
BERBERIS × OTTAWENSIS,
  B. THUNBERGII
CATALPA BIGNONIOIDES,
  C. BIGNONIOIDES 'AUREA',
  C. SPECIOSA
CORYLUS MAXIMA 'PURPUREA'
COTINUS COGGYGRIA,
  C. OBOVATUS
ERYTHRINA CRISTA-GALLI
EUCALYPTUS GUNNII
INDIGOFERA HETERANTHA
MELIANTHUS MAJOR
PAULOWNIA TOMENTOSA
PHILADELPHUS CORONARIUS
  'AUREUS'
PHLOMIS FRUTICOSA
POPULUS × CANDICANS 'AURORA'
RHUS TYPHINA 'DISSECTA'
SAMBUCUS RACEMOSA 'PLUMOSA
  AUREA'
  S. NIGRA 'GUINCHO PURPLE'
  S. RACEMOSA 'PLUMOSA AUREA'
TOONA SINENSIS 'FLAMINGO'

ENHANCING FOLIAGE

Trees and shrubs that are known to respond well to hard-pruning (*see left*) can be cut back hard every year to produce specimens with much larger or more colorful leaves. Good results rely on feeding with a balanced fertilizer in spring to provide nutrients to rebuild the growth removed.

Pot-trained foliage plant
If confined to a pot and hard-pruned in spring, Paulownia tomentosa *produces extra-large, exotic-looking leaves. Cut back to a woody framework and pare wounds cleanly (inset). Grow under glass in cool climates where flowering can be unreliable.*

RESTRICTING FORM

Trees that naturally produce very flexible wood, like apples, offer great potential for training and pruning to very "restricted" forms. The apple stepover, a variation of a cordon, is an extreme example. When bent horizontally, the dominance of the leading shoot is overcome, inducing many flowering and fruiting sideshoots or spurs. Use it to form a decorative and productive edging to beds in the kitchen garden.

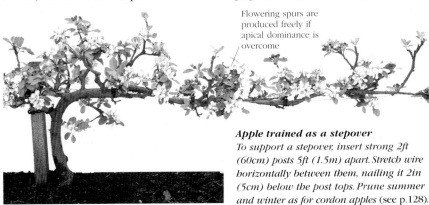

Flowering spurs are produced freely if apical dominance is overcome

Apple trained as a stepover
To support a stepover, insert strong 2ft (60cm) posts 5ft (1.5m) apart. Stretch wire horizontally between them, nailing it 2in (5cm) below the post tops. Prune summer and winter as for cordon apples (see p.128).

How to Cut Correctly

PRUNING CUTS SHOULD ALWAYS BE as small, clean, and neat as possible; the aim is to help the plant to heal its wounds rapidly. Young wood heals fastest, so prune shoots before they become woody and twigs before they become branches. Large wounds, especially those with torn or bruised tissue, allow easy access to disease-causing organisms.

Making cuts

A woody plant's natural defense system is at its strongest at the branch collar (a swelling where a branch joins the main trunk), at a fork on the branch, or at a node (bud or leaf joint). Bearing this in mind, do your best to make small, clean cuts at these points to speed natural healing. A slanting cut, if possible, is preferable, since rain cannot collect on a sloping surface. Water is a principal carrier of disease; many fungi and wood-rotting organisms spread by spores washed from the air and from nearby plant tissues by splashing raindrops.

CORRECT   TOO SLOPING   TOO HIGH   ROUGH CUT

Good and bad cuts
A correct cut is made at a gentle angle, ¼in (5mm) above a bud, sloping down away from it. Do not leave stubs or torn tissue, which will die back, or make steeply sloping cuts that breach the node's natural barrier.

Bud arrangements

All woody plants produce buds in one of two main patterns; these indicate how to make pruning cuts. Alternate buds arise at intervals, often in a spiral, along the sides of the stem. With these, it is possible to make the preferred sloping cut to the bud, from which one new shoot will grow. Opposite buds arise in pairs from the same point at a node. A sloping cut would damage one or both of the buds from which the new shoots will grow, so here, a neat, straight cut above the buds is the only option.

Alternate bud (left)
Make a slanting cut at a point ¼in (5mm) above the bud. A gentle slope allows moisture to roll off the cut surface and reduces the risk of disease.

Opposite buds (right)
Cut squarely across the shoot ¼in (5mm) above a node with a healthy pair of buds. Two strong, healthy shoots should then develop.

LARGER CUTS

Sometimes it is necessary to make larger pruning cuts, such as when removing the branch of a tree. These often take several growing seasons to heal, leaving potential entry points for disease. To reduce this risk, it is imperative to make cuts that heal with maximum speed. Make a smooth cut at the right point and scar tissue will grow from the edge to the center, sealing the wound and preventing entry of harmful organisms.

REMOVING A BRANCH

For thick wood, always use a powerful tool such as these sharp loppers

Clean cut
Protective new wood – callus or scar tissue – has formed rapidly with a clean cut.

Cutting to the branch collar
Make a clean cut just beyond the raised ring, or collar, at the base of the branch (see inset and p.11). This ensures that the wound does not interfere with sap flow up the main branch or trunk.

Rough cut
Fungal spores that cause rots and cavities have invaded torn and jagged tissue.

WHEN TO PRUNE

TREES
Most trees are pruned when dormant, from late autumn to late winter. The wounds heal quickly once strong growth begins in spring. Some trees, for example birches, "bleed" if cut as the sap is rising, or is about to do so, and so are not pruned between mid- to late winter and midsummer. Cherries, which are prone to silver-leaf disease, are pruned in summer when the risk of infection is lower (*see pp.136–7*).

SHRUBS
Deciduous shrubs that flower before midsummer bloom on wood made the previous year. Prune just after flowering to promote new growth. Those that bloom after midsummer flower on the current year's wood; prune in late winter or early spring. Evergreens are usually pruned in spring when danger of frost has passed but may be trimmed lightly after flowering to shape them or to remove old, flowered wood.

Tools for the Job

IT IS WELL WORTH buying the best tools that you can afford. Before you buy, make sure that the tools feel comfortable to use: check that they fit into your hand well, are easy to grip, and can be used without strain.

Cutting tools

The basic tools you will need for pruning are shears, pruners, and for heavier work, a pair of loppers or a long-handled tree pruner. Thicker branches are best cut with a saw. Use a pruning knife with a large down-swept blade to clean up any snags. Shears can be used on plants that need regular clipping, and for hedges and topiary. Always keep cutting blades sharp, and take care of your tools by cleaning and drying them after use. A final wipe with an oily rag will keep blades rust free and in good condition.

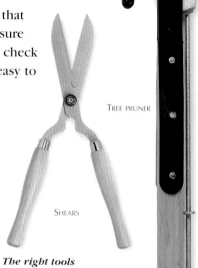

TREE PRUNER

SHEARS

The right tools
Ideally, have the appropriate tool at hand for every job. For best results, use a tool only for the tasks for which it was designed.

Using your tools correctly

Pruners can be used for all soft growth and on woody stems up to ½in (1cm) in diameter. Always use them the "right way up": the narrow, upper cutting blade should be nearer the bud or stem junction to which you are cutting so that the crushing effect of the thicker blade is confined to the tissue being removed. For thicker stems, to 1in (2.5cm), use a pair of loppers. A special pruning saw designed for garden use is ideal for larger jobs; household saws clog up quickly when cutting green wood.

USING PRUNERS CORRECTLY

Pruning correctly
Using the thin blade nearer the bud or stem junction (left) gives a clean, precise cut; reversing the position of the blades gives you less control and a tearing action (below left). Cutting an over-thick stem (below) blunts the blades and crushes stems.

USING PRUNERS INCORRECTLY

USING PRUNERS INCORRECTLY

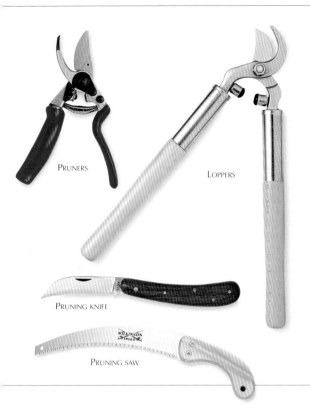

PRUNERS

LOPPERS

PRUNING KNIFE

PRUNING SAW

POWER TOOLS

Used with strict attention to safety, power tools are ideal for some tasks. A nylon-line trimmer makes short work of expanses of groundcover, and hedge trimmers are ideal for large hedges.

- Electric tools must be fitted with a ground fault circuit interrupter (GFCI) or circuit breaker to protect you if you should accidentally cut through the cord. Never trim wet plants, or work in wet weather.
- Protective goggles are essential with power tools, and earplugs are recommended.

PROTECTIVE GOGGLES

USING LOPPERS CORRECTLY

USING LOPPERS INCORRECTLY

Using loppers

A stem whose girth fits entirely within the bite of the loppers is easy to cut; the long handles exert extra leverage, so little effort is needed (far left). A stem or branch that is too wide for the blades strains the loppers; a single, clean cut is unlikely here (left).

Pruning saw and knife

A saw with a curved blade (pruning saw) is ideal for cutting thick wood or stubs in confined spaces (right). Use a sharp knife to trim any rough edges on cuts large or small; the curved blade of a pruning knife gives greater control (far right).

USING A PRUNING SAW

USING A KNIFE

ORNAMENTAL TREES

THE TREES that you plant in your garden form both
the elements of most structural importance and an
enduring legacy. A wide range of trees is available
to suit most growing conditions, including a good
selection of smaller trees, which are ideal for
relatively small modern gardens. Most need little
pruning or training once established, but the future
of a mature tree is often determined by the way
it is trained when young. It needs to have a
sturdy, well-balanced branch structure that will
remain safe and healthy into maturity and beyond,
as well as being pleasing to the eye. The
techniques of pruning, training, and grafting all
contribute to forming a sound structure that also
makes the most of a tree's ornamental virtues.

A beautifully formed tree *A tupelo tree will make an enduring contribution to the landscape.*

TREE FORMS

A WELL-GROWN TREE is trained when young to one of a number of forms. In most cases, training simply reinforces a natural habit, although sometimes, as with weeping standards, the shape is developed and maintained by pruning and training. To be sure that a tree does not outgrow its site, always check its final dimensions before planting.

CHOOSING A FORM

In the nursery industry, standardized descriptions of tree form and size are used to help buyers make their initial choice. As a tree matures, some of the rigid form distinction made in the nursery may be lost. This is seldom a problem unless the tree's structural safety is threatened; the tree will look no less pleasing as it assumes a more natural growth habit. But in very restricted forms, especially those like weeping standards that are top-grafted, careful control is needed if the ornamental effect is to be conserved.

Young trees

Training usually begins in a tree's second or third winter. In most cases, a very young tree consists of a single unbranched stem in its first year; this is known as a "maiden whip." Once side branches or laterals grow, usually in its second year, it is referred to as a "feathered" whip. Both of these forms can be purchased from speciality growers, so that you can train them yourself. When selecting a tree, make sure that the tree you have in mind is suitable for training in the form you would like. Always check that the tree's height and spread at maturity fits the chosen site. If the tree grows too large, your long-term investment is wasted, since it may have to be felled or endure costly tree surgery when it outgrows its allotted space.

Branched-head standard
Has a single, clear trunk that branches to form an open-centered crown. A common natural form, it can also be produced by top-grafting, or by cutting back a main stem to induce branching at a given height.

SUITABLE FOR
Albizia, Malus, Prunus cerasifera, Prunus × subhirtella, *and some other flowering cherries.*

Half-standard
Should have a clear trunk of 30-49in (75-125cm) and a compact crown of evenly spaced branches. The form is often lost with age, but a few trees, like bay, Laurus nobilis, can be pruned to retain these proportions.

SUITABLE FOR
Acer platanoides 'Brilliantissimum', Cornus kousa, Eucalyptus gunnii, Hoheria lyallii, Malus floribunda, Prunus serrula.

Feathered tree

The natural form of most young trees, with trunks clothed in branches almost to the ground. As they mature, many shed lower branches to develop into a central-leader standard.

SUITABLE FOR
Betula pendula, B. pubescens, Carpinus betulus, Carya, Cornus alternifolia, C. capitata, Ilex, Malus baccata.

Central-leader standard

Has a clear trunk of 5–6ft (1.5–2m) and a straight stem with a distinct leading shoot. A common form in nature, it can also be produced by removing the lower branches from a young feathered tree.

SUITABLE FOR
Aesculus hippocastanum, Alnus, Betula, Carpinus, Castanea, Crataegus, Davidia, Fagus, Fraxinus, Juglans, Laburnum, Liriodendron, Paulownia, Platanus, and many more.

Fastigiate tree

An entirely natural growth habit, producing a narrow crown of upswept branches from top to bottom. Cannot be formed by pruning and needs no pruning to maintain. Many conifers and poplars grow this way.

FOUND IN
Carpinus betulus 'Fastigiata', Eucryphia × nymansensis, Fagus sylvatica 'Dawyck', Populus nigra 'Italica', Prunus 'Amanogawa'.

Bush

Most commonly created for fruit trees, to produce low-growing, productive trees that are easy to harvest. To achieve this form, fruit trees are grafted onto a dwarfing rootstock. Seldom seen as a natural form, except in relatively small trees.

SUITABLE FOR
apples, pears, plums, sour cherries, quince, medlar, and mulberry.

Multistemmed tree

Branching low down, at or near ground-level, this form has several distinct stems or trunks and resembles a large shrub. A natural form, especially in trees reluctant to develop a single leader.

SUITABLE FOR
Celtis occidentalis, Cercis siliquastrum, Embothrium coccineum, Halesia, Nyssa sylvatica, Oxydendrum.

Weeping standard

Almost always produced by top-grafting, or grafting several buds at the top of a clear stem. A highly unnatural form needing maintenance pruning throughout its life. A few naturally weeping trees can be trained to this form.

SUITABLE FOR
Betula pendula 'Youngii', Fraxinus excelsior 'Pendula', Morus alba 'Pendula', Pyrus salicifolia, Salix caprea 'Kilmarnock'.

BUYING YOUNG TREES

TO GIVE A TREE the best possible start, choose a small, sturdy specimen, no more than two years old. A ready-trained three- or four-year-old tree may look like a better value, but it is more likely to suffer from postplanting shock after being moved, and fail to "grow away" well.

EARLY GROWTH

The ash tree (*near right*) is a good example of a well-trained tree at the end of its second growing season. Supported by a lightweight cane, it has a growing point at the apex of its single, straight shoot and is clothed with healthy leaves. The container is large enough to accommodate, without constriction, a root system capable of supporting the top-growth. (The spread of the tree should never be more than 3–4 times the width of its container). In contrast, the locust (*far right*) has developed two leading shoots that will probably create a structurally unsafe fork at maturity. There is too much top growth for the constricted roots to sustain, and the tree is unsupported and growing at an angle.

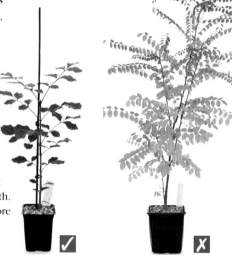

Well-trained and neglected specimens
The ash tree (left) *is upright, vigorous, and healthy, but the locust* (right) *is badly shaped and lopsided.*

GRAFTED TREES

Many tree cultivars are produced by grafting a scion – a selected cultivar (in the form of a bud or length of stem) – on a rootstock from a compatible plant. The "graft union" can usually be seen as a swelling near the base of the trunk. A tree produced by bud-grafting grows away from the graft point as a single shoot. Where a section of stem is used as the scion, its topmost side bud grows out to form the leading shoot. Any growth that appears below the graft union is from the rootstock – not the desirable cultivar – and must be removed completely as seen.

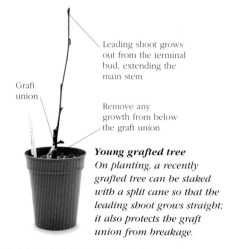

Leading shoot grows out from the terminal bud, extending the main stem

Graft union

Remove any growth from below the graft union

Young grafted tree
On planting, a recently grafted tree can be staked with a split cane so that the leading shoot grows straight; it also protects the graft union from breakage.

POT-GROWN AND BARE-ROOT TREES

If you can, select and collect young trees in person, so that you can assess nursery conditions and look trees over for potential problems (see opposite and below).Transport them carefully, under cover or wraps. A tree transported on an open truck or roof rack, for example, with its foliage buffeted in the wind, suffers considerable stress. Bare-root trees are particularly vulnerable to damage during lifting and transporting. Exposed to the air, the fine feeder roots begin to dry out and die. Generally, the roots of container-grown or root-balled trees do not need pruning when transplanting, but remedial action may be necessary with root-balled trees if damage has occurred. Before planting, cleanly cut away roots with ragged, broken ends or abrasions. Prune misshapen or lopsided roots so that there is a good spread emanating from the stem.

Selecting trees for purchase (below)
This short, sturdy, well-trained young tree has a good balance between top-growth and root growth.The stem is clear, and the young side branches are well-spaced and at the correct wide V-angle with the main stem.

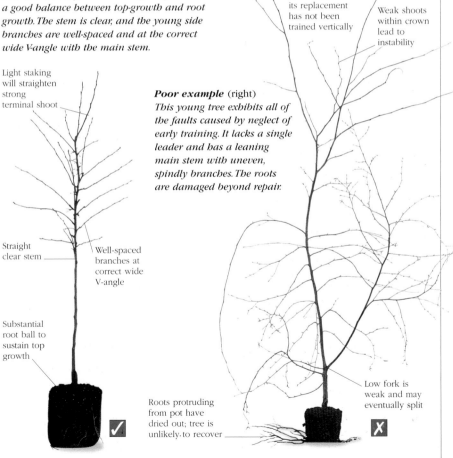

Light staking
will straighten
strong
terminal shoot

Straight
clear stem

Well-spaced
branches at
correct wide
V-angle

Substantial
root ball to
sustain top
growth

Poor example (right)
This young tree exhibits all of the faults caused by neglect of early training. It lacks a single leader and has a leaning main stem with uneven, spindly branches.The roots are damaged beyond repair.

Original leader
has failed, and
its replacement
has not been
trained vertically

Weak shoots
within crown
lead to
instability

Low fork is
weak and may
eventually split

Roots protruding
from pot have
dried out; tree is
unlikely to recover

THE EARLY YEARS

IF NOT ALREADY in its final site, a two-year-old tree can be planted out and
formative training can continue *in situ*, without further disturbance to
the root system. For most trees, the best form to choose is simply a well-
shaped version of the habit the tree would naturally adopt, because this
is the most likely to remain structurally sound until maturity.

FEATHERED TREES

Most evergreens are grown as feathered
trees; the majority develop a neat conical
shape naturally. The pruning of evergreens
is done from late summer to before
midwinter. A feathered tree is by far the
easiest form to produce, since it requires
little pruning other than to remove dead,

diseased, or damaged wood. Check regularly
for crossing shoots and cut them out. Look
for shoots that form a narrow angle of
attachment to the trunk and remove them
too. The junction will be weak and in time
may result in heavy branches splitting from
the trunk at this point.

Years 1, 2, and 3, winter
*Cut off laterals at a narrow angle to the trunk
and any that are not well spaced or positioned.
If laterals grow more strongly on one side,
tip-prune weaker shoots to stimulate growth.*

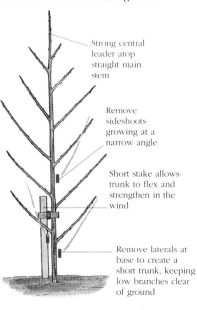

Leader continues
strong upward
growth

Remove or cut back
to one bud any
vertical shoots that
may compete with
the leader

Strong central
leader atop
straight main
stem

Remove
sideshoots
growing at a
narrow angle

Short stake allows
trunk to flex and
strengthen in the
wind

Remove laterals at
base to create a
short trunk, keeping
low branches clear
of ground

Check tie,
loosen if
necessary;
remove
stake when
tree is
firmly
established

Remove any
regrowth at
stem base

YEAR 1

YEARS 2 AND 3

CENTRAL-LEADER STANDARD

A central-leader standard has a length of clear trunk, topped by a crown through which the leader persists. Many trees take this form naturally; the lower branches die back and are shed as they are "shaded out" by the increasing density of branches above. The main danger in this form of training is that the leader may be damaged or lost because another shoot overtakes it. Both of these problems can be rectified if remedial action is performed promptly (*see p.37*).

CLEARING THE TRUNK

The trunks of all standards are cleared in the same way, gradually over several years. If laterals are stripped away all at once, dormant buds break low down on the stem, producing unwanted shoots and inhibiting top growth. If removed when small, they leave little scarring. Another reason for removing laterals in stages is that their foliage helps to provide the tree with energy; laterals temporarily retained are known as "stem builders."

Years 1, 2, 3, and 4, winter

As a guide to clearing the trunk in stages, visualize the trunk, from the ground to the topmost lateral, divided approximately into thirds. To remove laterals, make small cuts that do not breach the branch collar (see p.11); the swelling will be very slight, if visible at all, so leave a stub of no more than ¼in (5mm). If shortening laterals, make correctly angled cuts to a healthy, outward-facing bud.

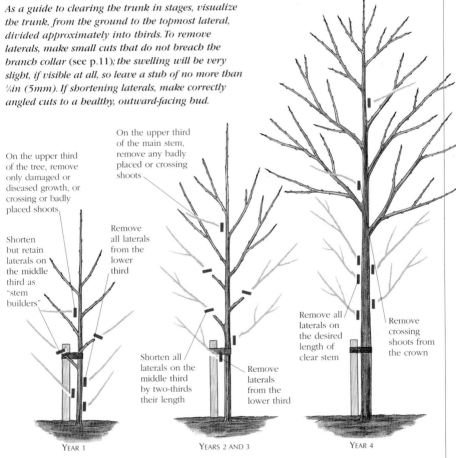

On the upper third of the tree, remove only damaged or diseased growth, or crossing or badly placed shoots

On the upper third of the main stem, remove any badly placed or crossing shoots

Shorten but retain laterals on the middle third as "stem builders"

Remove all laterals from the lower third

Shorten all laterals on the middle third by two-thirds their length

Remove laterals from the lower third

Remove all laterals on the desired length of clear stem

Remove crossing shoots from the crown

YEAR 1

YEARS 2 AND 3

YEAR 4

BRANCHED-HEAD STANDARD

Branched-head standards do occur naturally; for example, many oaks adopt this habit with age, as the leader loses dominance. Pruning to form a branched head is used on trees that otherwise grow to considerable height, although this becomes less necessary, or possible, on older trees, which may tend to revert to upward growth. Training in the first and second years is the same as for a central-leader standard (*see p.33*).

BRANCHED-HEAD STANDARD

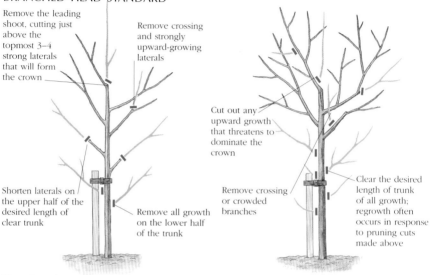

Remove the leading shoot, cutting just above the topmost 3–4 strong laterals that will form the crown

Remove crossing and strongly upward-growing laterals

Shorten laterals on the upper half of the desired length of clear trunk

Remove all growth on the lower half of the trunk

Cut out any upward growth that threatens to dominate the crown

Remove crossing or crowded branches

Clear the desired length of trunk of all growth; regrowth often occurs in response to pruning cuts made above

Year 3 or 4, winter
When 3–4 strong laterals have developed above the required length of clear trunk, remove the leader to create a branched head.

Year 4 or 5, winter
Check the overall shape before cutting, then make pruning cuts to restore or maintain a balanced, open-centered crown.

FORMING A LABURNUM TUNNEL

Plant one- or two-year-old feathered laburnum trees at 6–10ft (2–3m) intervals. Train over the arch, tying in early in the season while the wood is still supple. If insufficient laterals are produced to fill the spaces, tip back the leading shoot to encourage laterals to break. At the end of each subsequent growing season, reduce all laterals to within 2–3 buds of the main framework branches to encourage formation of flowering wood.

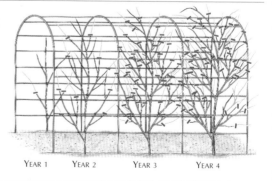

YEAR 1   YEAR 2   YEAR 3   YEAR 4

WEEPING STANDARDS

There are two types of weeping standard: natural, and grafted. Trees that weep naturally first grow upward, if well staked, then arch at a height that depends on the species. With top-grafted standards, such as *Salix caprea* 'Kilmarnock', the branches all tend to grow away in the same horizontal plane, and the crown becomes congested. To avoid this, remove any shoots that cross the center at awkward angles early on; because upward growth spoils the weeping form, remove that too. Always remove any shoots growing on the clear stem; they are from the rootstock. Staking with a tall, strong stake is usually required for some years after the head has developed. The crown of a weeping tree often grows rapidly and may prove too heavy to be supported by the trunk until it has increased greatly in girth. Without support, there is a risk of the entire crown being blown out in strong winds.

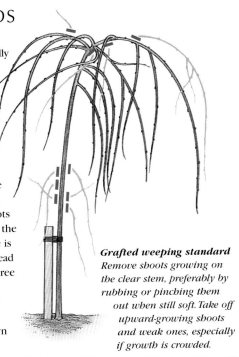

Grafted weeping standard
Remove shoots growing on the clear stem, preferably by rubbing or pinching them out when still soft. Take off upward-growing shoots and weak ones, especially if growth is crowded.

NATURAL WEEPING STANDARDS

Some naturally weeping standards, like this *Betula pendula* 'Tristis', may form a squat, low-spreading mound unless trained firmly to the vertical in the early years. It is essential to support the leading shoot's upward growth until the wood has hardened enough for the stem to remain rigid. As the tree grows and while the leading shoot is still flexible, attach the leader to a vertical cane lashed to the main stake. Keep tying in until the leader reaches the required height; in this way the height of the trunk may be extended to about 12ft (4m). The weeping habit can then be allowed to develop naturally.

Raising the height of the main stem
Careful vertical training of the main stem to the required height allows branches to weep freely rather than trail on the ground.

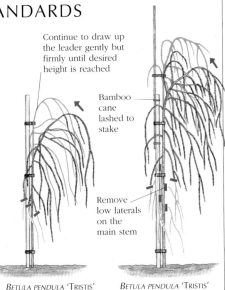

Continue to draw up the leader gently but firmly until desired height is reached

Bamboo cane lashed to stake

Remove low laterals on the main stem

BETULA PENDULA 'TRISTIS'
YEARS 1 AND 2

BETULA PENDULA 'TRISTIS'
YEAR 3 UNTIL ESTABLISHED

MULTISTEMMED TREE ON A LOW TRUNK

Some trees, like this maple *Acer davidii*, are grown for their attractive bark. They are often pruned to produce a multistemmed specimen on a short trunk to display more of the bark's striations. Maples "bleed" sap so are pruned when fully dormant, in winter. When young, they are prone to dieback and cold damage. Small cuts can be made to remove damage in late summer, but leave more substantial cuts until winter pruning.

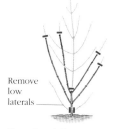

Remove low laterals

Cut weak laterals to a bud at 1–2in (2.5–5cm)

Remove lower shoots to clear main stems

Year 1, winter
Prune to 20in (50cm), above 2 pairs of strong shoots. Tip-prune these by 4in (10cm).

Year 2, winter
Cut back dead or damaged wood to a healthy bud. Prune any weak shoots hard.

Year 3, winter
Keep main stems clear of low laterals; remove inward-facing laterals to open the center.

MULTISTEMMED FORM FROM A SINGLE STEM

This method is also used to display beautiful bark, but unlike the form shown above, is never used on grafted trees. It can be used to enhance the form of naturally multistemmed or low branching trees; by restricting the number of stems and inward-growing laterals, a thicket is avoided. Some trees, like *Celtis*, may not form a single stem in regions with cool summers, but are equally attractive when grown as multistemmed forms.

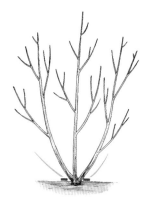

Year 1, winter
Cut back the stem of a 2-year-old tree straight across at 3in (8cm) above ground level.

Year 2, winter
Select 3–4 strong, well-spaced shoots to create a framework and remove the remainder.

Year 3, winter
Let laterals develop; remove any suckers and low laterals if clear stems are wanted.

TROUBLESHOOTING

If neglected, trees may produce two or more leading shoots in competition with each other, which must be dealt with if a central-leader specimen is desired. On this young tree (*right*), several shoots are clustered at the tree's apex. If all are allowed to develop, they will compromise the tree's structural stability at maturity. The topmost shoot will not always be the best choice as a leader; select the strongest and most upright shoot.

Competing leaders
Where competing leaders have formed (right), select the strongest upright shoot. The topmost shoot may now not make the best new leader (inset); here, the lower shoot is stronger and straighter. Shorten vigorous low shoots by one-third to half of their length.

This strong, upright shoot is the best candidate to become the new leader

BROKEN LEADERS

If the leading shoot of the tree is "lost" – it dies back, is damaged by cold, or is broken – prune it back to the nearest sound, strong lateral that can be trained vertically to take its place. If no laterals have yet emerged, prune to a healthy bud, and then train the resulting shoot.

Attach new leader to cane

Cut back damaged leader

1 *Select a new leader and attach it to a vertical cane with soft twine at intervals of 10in (25cm).*

2 *Carefully cut the broken shoot with an angled cut, taking care not to damage the new leader.*

DUAL LEADERS

On trees with opposite buds, the loss of a leader results in a pair of new ones. Select the shoot most easily trained to the line of the original main-stem (here the right-hand shoot), and remove its competitor.

TWO LEADERS FROM OPPOSITE BUDS

STAKING

ALL BUT THE SMALLEST whips or young feathered trees need the support of a stake for the first two years until a strong trunk and good root system are established. The purpose of a stake is *not* to hold the tree up but to allow it to develop a straight, vertical stem. Flexing in the wind is necessary to strengthen the trunk, and in most cases, a short stake and looser ties that permit this is the preferred option. There are a number of staking methods to choose from to suit the size and type of tree, the density of its crown, and the degree of exposure in the planting site.

SINGLE STAKES AND TIES

When planting a bare-root tree, insert the stake into the hole first and spread the roots around it – never drive a stake through the root system. For a straight stake (*see below, left and right*), insert on the side of the prevailing wind so that the stem is pushed away from the stake. With a short angled stake (*below, center*), lean it into the prevailing wind. Drive stakes at least 24in

(60cm) into the ground. Ties must hold the tree securely but not tightly and should be used with a spacer so that neither tie nor stake rubs against young bark; abrasions may affect the future health of the tree. Check ties regularly and loosen as the tree's girth expands; if they constrict the stem, the nutrient supply to the crown is reduced and may eventually be cut off if the bark is girdled.

Low, straight stake
A stake that is less than one-third of the tree's height permits strengthening by flexing. Use a tie and spacer to avoid chafing young bark.

Low, angled stake
Useful in exposed sites. Lean at 45° into prevailing winds, and attach by a belt tie in a figure eight to avoid chafing the bark.

Tall, straight stake
Tall stakes with a tie and spacer are useful in the case of top-grafted trees or standards with dense, heavy, or weeping crowns.

TWO-STAKE SYSTEM

A pair of short stakes, driven into the bottom of the planting hole on either side of the root ball, can be used for most trees. This system is ideal for root-ball or container-grown trees; the stakes can be placed so that there is little risk that they will penetrate and damage roots. The tree is secured with looped rubber ties nailed to the stake, which allow the tree to flex freely in the wind, thus strengthening the trunk.

Pair of short stakes

A young tree is well supported by low stakes on either side of the root ball and secured by soft rubber strips that enable the tree to flex freely in the wind.

GUY-WIRES

A single stake is inadequate if planting a large tree. A sizable crown effectively forms a sail and may blow out in strong wind, often snapping just at the top of a single stake. Guy-wires provide evenly distributed support until root growth is sufficient to support the weight of the crown, usually after two growing seasons. Guide the strong wire through low, sturdy forks in the crown of the tree and attach to angled stakes.

Stabilizing a large tree

Thread the wire through lengths of hosepipe (left) to protect the bark. Use angled stakes fitted with wire turnbuckles (below and inset) so that the trunk is trained vertically.

ESTABLISHED TREES

ALTHOUGH ESTABLISHED TREES do not need regular pruning, all benefit from regular health checks throughout their lives to identify and then remove dead, diseased, or damaged wood. For most, the time to check and correct defects is in late summer and midwinter. A few, like top-grafted weeping standards or those with variegated foliage, require more attention to correct defects, relieve congestion, or remove reverted shoots.

UNEVEN GROWTH

The most common cause of uneven growth is suppression by neighboring trees or other shade-casting structures. If the prime cause remains in place, there is little point in remedial pruning. If, however, the offending structure is removed, the tree may be restored over several years. In the first year, prune weak branches hard and take off all suckers and dead, diseased, and crossing wood. In the second and subsequent years, reduce any overcrowding (which may result from the previous year's cuts) and remove or shorten other branches to enhance the shape. Remove only one or two branches in any one year; take them out in sections to reduce risk of tearing the bark (*see opposite*).

Year 1, winter
Tip-prune branch leaders on the stronger side to produce limited regrowth. Cut back the weaker side hard to stimulate vigorous regrowth that will balance the tree's form.

Year 2 onward, winter
Strong new shoots have grown on the weaker side. In this and subsequent seasons, remove crossing shoots and any that will spoil the crown's symmetry if allowed to develop.

CUTTING OFF A BRANCH

You should remove only those branches that are no higher than shoulder height and are light enough for you to support safely. For your own- and the tree's - safety, any major pruning that has to be done from a ladder or involves removal of large branches should be undertaken by a professional arborist.

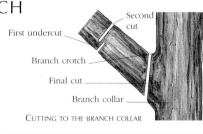

Second cut

First undercut

Branch crotch

Final cut

Branch collar

CUTTING TO THE BRANCH COLLAR

1 *Reduce the weight of the branch first. About 12in (30cm) from the trunk, saw a quarter of the way into the branch from the underside, to avoid the bark tearing if the branch breaks.*

2 *Cut squarely down from the top of the branch, 2in (5cm) beyond the undercut, until the section falls away. The final cut should now be much more controllable.*

3 *Make the final cut just beyond the branch collar, at an equal and opposite angle to that made by the branch's bark ridge (see p.11), to avoid damaging the tree.*

4 *Smooth any rough edges with a pruning knife. Wound paints are no longer recommended because they can interfere with the tree's natural healing.*

THINNING REGROWTH

Hard pruning often results in the production of fast-growing shoots, known as epicormic or water shoots, from dormant buds under the bark around the site of the pruning wound. If left, they proliferate and divert energy from the rest of the tree and seldom make safe and robust new branches. If they are carefully reduced in number, however, it can do much to improve the appearance of an awkward-looking, truncated stub.

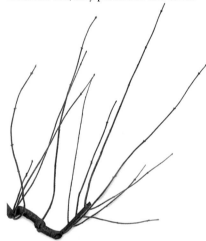

Selected shoots are shortened back to a healthy bud

All surplus buds and wayward shoots have been removed

Before
This damaged branch has been lopped, giving it a clumsy appearance. However, many new shoots have appeared; by careful selection, balanced regrowth can be developed.

After
Four strong shoots have been selected to create an open structure; each now has plenty of room to develop. Shorten them by at least half, varying lengths to avoid a "mop-head" cluster.

WITCHES' BROOM

Many trees develop dense clusters of stunted twigs and foliage on their branches, usually as a response to infection by mites, insects, or fungi. These witches' brooms, as they are known, are harmless to the tree but often look unsightly clustered in the crown, especially on trees of open, airy habit like silver birches (*Betula pendula*). The affected branches can be removed at their point of origin, or to a suitable point below the affected area, at the junction of a main branch, for example. This is best done when the tree is fully dormant and the witches' brooms can clearly be seen.

Witches' broom
Clusters of twiggy stunted growth can enhance a gnarled, picturesque appearance in a tree, but they can be removed if found unsightly.

MAJOR SURGERY

On large trees, especially in urban areas, major tree surgery is an extremely dangerous task that should be carried out only by a qualified tree surgeon (arborist). The work may involve crown reduction to reduce the overall size of a mature tree's canopy that has outgrown its space; this procedure is often done in conjunction with crown thinning to remove congested growth. Crown lifting is used to remove the lower branches of a large tree that overhang and obstruct a path, driveway, or public highway, but may also be used to open up a view or admit more light to allow plantings beneath. These operations are seldom necessary where proper species selection has been carried out in the first place; *always* check a tree's mature dimensions before planting.

LEGAL PRECAUTIONS

■ It is essential, before any work is done, to check whether a tree is legally protected. If it is, you must obtain permission from the relevant local authority before felling or even pruning branches.

■ If tree work is likely to affect overhead wires or underground cables and pipes, the relevant utility provider must be informed, and the work carried out by a professional arborist.

■ The most bitter disputes between neighbors often arise from misunderstandings over boundaries. It is both wise and courteous to advise neighbors of your intentions if your tree borders their property; cooperation is essential if you must prune a neighbor's tree that encroaches on your garden. You are legally entitled to remove only as much of a branch that grows over a line drawn vertically upward from your boundary. The cuttings are the property of the neighbors.

Crown lifting
Lower branches that obstruct free passage beneath them, block out light, or obscure road signs or street lights are removed to create a longer length of clear trunk.

Crown thinning and reduction
Thinning the canopy admits light and air to the center of the crown; crown reduction reduces the height and spread of a tree, for example, to permit passage of power lines.

CONIFERS

MOST CONIFERS ARE cone-bearing evergreens with needle- or scalelike leaves, and have strongly upright and dominant leaders that give rise to a typical conical habit. With few exceptions, they are best grown with minimal pruning. When mature, pruning is best avoided altogether unless to repair damage or remove reverted or wayward growth.

TRAINING A LEADER

The majority of conifers will naturally re-form a leading shoot if damaged when young or in early maturity. If damage occurs, select and train in a new leader as soon as possible. If injury occurs in later life, dual leaders often result. It is essential to remove one of them to produce a single-stemmed tree and to avoid dangerous narrow forks at maturity. Timing is critical, since most conifers are resinous and bleed profusely when cut. Pruning in autumn or midwinter keeps bleeding to a minimum.

Competing leader
To maintain a single-stemmed, central-leader tree, cut out the weaker or more crooked shoot cleanly at its base.

REPLACING A BROKEN LEADER

1 *On young plants, a broken leader can be replaced with a strong lateral that can be tied in to assume the dominant role.*

2 *Remove all damaged growth, cutting it back cleanly to a strong, preferably upright, shoot. The resulting small wound will heal quickly.*

3 *Tie the new leader to a stake pushed through the tree's center. Remove the stake once the new leader is growing strongly upward.*

SPLAYED SHOOTS

Wind, snow, or ice, or occasionally the weight of an upright branch, can cause growth to splay out, spoiling the form of the tree (*see inset, right*). First check that the branch has not split; if it is undamaged, it can be tied back into the main shoot.

Dealing with splayed-out growth
Tie in undamaged shoots to the main stem, using soft material in case the tie is forgotten. Tarred twine or nylon tights are ideal.

DEAD PATCHES

Scorched or dead foliage should be removed completely (see *inset, right*). Unless damage is very minimal this leaves an unsightly hole, especially in formally shaped trees or hedges. New growth will not shoot from old wood, so disguise damage by tying in adjacent shoots across the hole, securing them with a stake tied to a main stem or branch.

Covering dead patches
Attach a stake to a main stem or branch. Draw neighboring branches over the gap and tie them in. New growth will hide the stake.

DWARF CONIFERS

Dwarf conifers are propagated from sports (natural mutations) of the "normal" tree. Sports are often selected for a dense, prostrate, or upright habit. Pruning is usually unnecessary, but sometimes a shoot reverts to the normal habit, which spoils the form and may eventually become dominant. All reverted growth must be cut out to maintain the distinctive shape for which the plant has been selected.

Removing reverted growth
The strongly upright shoot in this prostrate plant is removed at the point of origin, thus masking the cut within remaining foliage.

COPPICING AND POLLARDING

THE TRADITIONAL WOODLAND TECHNIQUES of coppicing and pollarding are similar and consist of hard pruning on a routine basis. Some trees respond to such treatment by producing vigorous new growth that is highly ornamental, such as larger than normal leaves or young stems in beautiful colors. These techniques are also used to restrict the size of large trees.

COPPICING

This entails the regular, sometimes annual, cutting back of a tree to ground level, when dormant, to obtain vigorous young stems. The tree has a full-sized root system, so regrowth of young, often richly colored, stems is vigorous, and leaves may be much larger or more colorful. Cutting to a low stump also makes it feasible to provide winter protection such as a mulch of straw to slightly tender trees like eucalyptus. Not all trees respond well to such hard pruning.

Pollarded* Acer negundo *'Flamingo'
Cut back hard to a low framework in winter for larger leaves (see below) *and a shrubby habit to suit confined spaces.*

Pruning for foliage effect
By being pollarded to a very low stem, this Acer negundo *'Flamingo' has responded by producing fresh, cream-splashed variegated foliage. Many trees develop the most attractive foliage on the newest growth.*

TREES AND SHRUBS

The following respond well to coppicing and pollarding:

ACER PENSYLVANICUM
 'ERYTHROCLADUM' (red stems)
AILANTHUS (large leaves)
CATALPA BIGNONIOIDES (large
 leaves)
CERCIS (flowers at eye level,
 but do not cut every year)
CORNUS ALBA (colored stems)
CORYLUS AVELLANA, C. MAXIMA
 'PURPUREA' (multistems and
 large leaves)
EUCALYPTUS (juvenile leaves)
FAGUS SYLVATICA (multistemmed)
PAULOWNIA (large leaves)
RHUS TYPHINA (large leaves)
RUBUS COCKBURNIANUS,
 R. THIBETANUS (colored stems)
SALIX ALBA and subspecies
 VITELLINA (colored stems)
TILIA PLATYPHYLLOS 'RUBRA'
 (red stems)

POLLARDING

Pollarding is much like coppicing, except that stems are cut back above a clear length of trunk. Willows and dogwoods are often pollarded to produce crops of young, vividly colored stems in shades of yellow, green, or scarlet. When leafless, they provide welcome winter color, growing to a height that displays the stems above other plantings. Stems are cut back before growth resumes in spring, securing the longest possible display. The technique is also effective in producing larger, more colorful leaves at eye level, or in maintaining eucalyptus, for example, in a state of perpetual youth: its juvenile leaves are often more attractive than adult ones. Pollarding is also used to restrict the size of large trees, such as lindens (*Tilia*), producing a compact crown that is ideal for a street tree. Both coppicing and pollarding are simple methods, but only a limited number of trees will tolerate such hard treatment: disease resistance is crucial to enable continual recovery from wounds.

***Established pollard* (Salix)**
Every 2-3 years, in late winter, cut back young stems to within ¾in (2cm) of the main stem.

Pollarded* Catalpa bignonioides *'Aurea'
This tree, suffering from dieback, was pollarded in winter to a framework of 4-5 branches on a 4ft (1.2m) trunk (left). New growth bears a crop of larger, more colorful leaves (right).

WINTER

SUMMER

HEDGES

WHETHER FORMAL OR INFORMAL, hedges perform several important roles in a garden. Hedges give structure and often form a backdrop to other plantings. They offer privacy, and provide shelter from strong winds and sun as well as filter out noise and dust from nearby roads. They can also, if suitable species are chosen, create a haven for wildlife.

STARTING A HEDGE

Prepare a band of ground 3ft (1m) wide and plant 1-2ft (30-60cm) apart, in a straight line, alternating weak and strong plants. Shorten strong leaders and laterals by one-third and weak shoots by two-thirds. Cut back vigorous species like hawthorn to 6-12in (15-30cm) to encourage a bushy base.

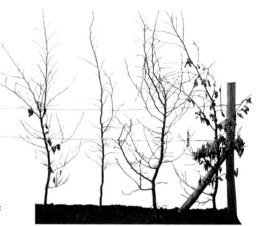

Providing support
New hedges need little support, except in exposed areas, when low wires and posts on the windward side may be necessary.

FORMAL HEDGES

Plants used for formal hedges must have a dense habit and tolerate close clipping. From the early stages, the sides should be cut at a slight angle (known as the "slope"), with the base as the widest point, to produce a tapered outline, with a flat or gently rounded top. This makes the hedge less vulnerable to damage by snow or strong winds, and allows more even distribution of light from the top to the bottom.

Tapered top
The shape of this hornbeam hedge permits light to reach the lower flanks, thus reducing foliage loss at the base.

Classic A-shape
This yew has been cut into a classic formal A-shape, which tapers gently to a neat, flat top.

Rounded top
Sloping sides and a rounded top give this conifer hedge a softer outline and also reduce damage from wind and snow.

SHAPING FORMAL HEDGES

The aim of pruning and training is to insure dense growth from the base to the top, and to produce a neat outline with a slope. When shaping, use a line or template as your guide; it is almost impossible to do this accurately by eye except on dwarf hedges, which look best with vertical sides. For most conifers and evergreens, only the laterals are pruned in the formative years. Do not shape the top until the desired height is reached.

Using a line
To achieve a level top, stretch taut string horizontally between two upright posts to act as a guideline for the highest part of the hedge, and cut the top along this line.

Using a template
To taper the top, cut a template (inset) of the required shape. Place on the hedge and cut following the line of the template, moving it along as you proceed; then cut the sides.

TRIMMING FORMAL HEDGES

Once the size and slope have been achieved, a hedge simply needs trimming to maintain its form, using a straightedge or garden line as a guide. Frequency, degree, and timing of trimming depends on species. Most hedges are cut twice annually: when dormant and in midsummer for deciduous hedges; in late spring and late summer for evergreens. For conifer hedges, regular trimming is essential; few conifers break freely from old wood.

Using shears or trimmers
Keep blades parallel to the line of the hedge to be sure top and sides are cut level and flat. Use a trimmer with a sweeping action to avoid cutting into the hedge and spoiling the shape.

INFORMAL HEDGES

An informal hedge is basically a screen of close-planted small trees or, more often, shrubs. Timing and techniques of pruning are much the same as for individual specimens and should be accompanied by gentle shaping of the outline. Remove over-long or misplaced growths, and trim back annually to keep within bounds. Trim large-leaved evergreens with pruners; shearing will damage individual leaves, which then become brown and unsightly. For flowering or fruiting hedges, timing is critical if the display is not to be spoiled. The easiest to manage are shrubs like *Pyracantha* (*see p.65*) or *Chaenomeles*, which bear their flowers on laterals or spurs from older wood, rather than terminally on growth that will be removed by trimming.

Flowering hedges
Garrya elliptica (left) *can be clipped as soon as the catkins fade. Most other flowering hedges that bloom before midsummer are cut after flowering; those that flower from midsummer on may be pruned when dormant or in spring.*

Semiformal and informal hedges
Shape gently with pruners. Cut back individual shoots to within the foliage canopy to disguise pruning wounds.

CONIFER HEDGES

Regular trimming of conifer hedges is essential to maintain a dense surface. If neglected, the usual result is a bare, woody center with a fringe of foliage at the extremities. Such hedges are both unsightly and prone to splitting or collapse in heavy snow or strong winds. While minor localized damage can be remedied by tying branches over small gaps (*see p.45*), in the long term, replacement is the best option for a badly neglected conifer hedge.

Section through a conifer hedge
Regularly trimmed conifers have a dense, even surface but are leafless within; most will not produce new shoots from old bare wood.

RENOVATING HEDGES

Even well-maintained hedges may gradually edge their way beyond bounds. Beech, hornbeam, hawthorn, holly, and yew all respond well to hard pruning. Renovate deciduous hedges in midwinter and evergreen ones in spring. Cut the top and each side in different years to avoid undue stress, reducing to at least 6in (15cm) less than the desired height and width. Feed and mulch well in spring after each pruning.

Renovated surface has produced dense regrowth

Second side is now cut back hard

Reducing hedge width, first year
Cut one side of the hedge back hard (right side), almost to the main stems if necessary. Prune the other side (left) as usual.

Reducing hedge width, second year
The renovated surface has produced dense regrowth. Cut the remaining surface back hard, by the same amount as the other side.

REDUCING HEIGHT

To re-create a dense, even top, reduce the height to at least 6in (15cm) below the desired height. If upper portions are very patchy, cut back even harder. Use a straightedge or garden line as a guide, insuring that all plants are cut to the same height. Feed and mulch well after pruning; regrowth should disguise wounds within one or two seasons.

Leggy hedges
Thin, gappy top growth is unsightly and reduces the hedge's effectiveness.

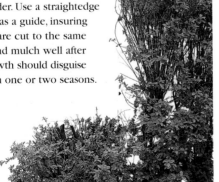

PLANTS FOR HEDGES

FORMAL HEDGES
ACER CAMPESTRE, BUXUS, CARPINUS BETULUS, CHAMAECYPARIS, CRATAEGUS MONOGYNA, ELAEAGNUS, FAGUS SYLVATICA, ESCALLONIA, GRISELINIA, ILEX, LAURUS, LONICERA NITIDA, PRUNUS LAUROCERASUS, P. LUSITANICA, TAXUS BACCATA, THUJA PLICATA
FLOWERING OR FRUITING HEDGES
CHAENOMELES, FORSYTHIA, FUCHSIA, POTENTILLA FRUTICOSA, PYRACANTHA, RIBES, ROSA
INFORMAL HEDGES
AUCUBA, BERBERIS, CORYLUS, COTONEASTER, GARRYA, OLEARIA, PRUNUS CERASIFERA 'PISSARDII', P. CERASIFERA 'NIGRA', TAMARIX.

TOPIARY

A FORM OF TRAINING to create living "sculpture," topiary is a garden art traditionally used to produce a variety of geometric forms. Shapes such as cones, obelisks, and columns provide a strong structural element in a design, and are ideal for framing a vista or as a contrasting foil for looser plantings.

Shapes and effects
Eyecatching forms are created by combining simple pruning and training; these need precise clipping and regular maintenance.

SPIRAL STEM   POODLE   BASIC CONE

CLIPPING TO CREATE SHAPES

The simplest topiary design is one close to the natural form of the plant. Plants used for topiary must have a dense habit, produce pliable growth, and respond well to close clipping. If a compact surface and sharp outline are required, they should also have small leaves. The species must be suitable for your soil type and climate; precise forms are quickly spoiled by dieback caused by cold and wind or unsuitable soil conditions.

Clip shoots back to a strong pair of buds. Avoid cutting individual leaves

1 *In the first year, a young boxwood tree is clipped roughly to shape. This will encourage the necessary dense, bushy growth.*

2 *Using a tripod of stakes and wire hoops as a guide, in the second year the bush is clipped into a neat, crisp cone with a dense surface.*

3 *In subsequent years, the finished plant is clipped two or three times a year, depending on growth rate, to retain a well-defined outline.*

MOP-HEAD STANDARD

A ready-trained mop-head standard like this bay tree (*Laurus nobilis*) is expensive to buy, but it is relatively easy to create. Prune a young, straight-stemmed plant back to a cluster of sideshoots at the top of the stem, shortening these to outward-facing buds. Clear shoots from the stem. Keep the stem clear by rubbing off any new buds that emerge. As new shoots develop, tip-prune each to a bud facing in the desired direction, to build up a dense, compact head.

Tip-prune shoots

Stem cleared of shoots

Remove basal suckers

YEAR 1

YEAR 2

Standard bay tree
Where not hardy, standard bay trees will need winter protection. If pot-grown, they can easily be moved into a cool greenhouse.

STEM EFFECTS

A mop-head standard of bay or weeping fig (*Ficus benjamina*) can be enhanced by special stem effects. Stems are easily braided when young; they eventually fuse together but will need support until growth hardens.

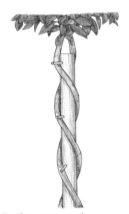

Barley sugar twist
Train one or two stems around a sturdy wooden pole, looping the stems under dowel pegs inserted in a spiral along its length. The pole is removed as growth hardens.

Braided stem
Form a braided stem simply by braiding together three flexible shoots. Select the strongest three on a multi-stemmed young plant, and remove the remainder.

SHRUBS FOR TOPIARY

A number of trees and shrubs are suitable for topiary work. When clipping larger-leaved species, like *Prunus lusitanica* or *Laurus nobilis*, be careful not to cut individual leaves.

ARTEMISIA ABROTANUM
BERBERIS
BUXUS MICROPHYLLA,
 B. SEMPERVIRENS
CRATAEGUS
CUPRESSUS SEMPERVIRENS
ELAEAGNUS ANGUSTIFOLIA,
 E. FORTUNEI
FICUS BENJAMINA
ILEX AQUIFOLIUM,
 I. CRENATA
JUNIPERUS
LAURUS NOBILIS
LIGUSTRUM OVALIFOLIUM
LONICERA NITIDA
MYRTUS COMMUNIS
OSMANTHUS
PRUNUS LUSITANICA
SANTOLINA CHAMAECYPARISSUS
TEUCRIUM CHAMAEDRYS
TAXUS

ORNAMENTAL SHRUBS

SOME OF THE MOST striking planting plans rely
on carefully chosen shrubs whose shapely form
and healthy growth give pleasure all year round.
Light pruning to shape and the routine removal of
dead, diseased, or damaged wood may be all that
some shrubs need to remain handsome and
vigorous. However, for many popular shrubs,
regular pruning is needed to enhance and
maintain the quality of their ornamental features
such as flowering and fruiting. Observe carefully
when and where on their branches these shrubs
flower and on what age of wood. Your aim, then,
is to remove old, unproductive wood in favor of
the young, vigorous, and fruitful, thus encouraging
the natural process of renewal.

Fragrant Philadelphus *Most* Philadelphus *need regular pruning to maximize flowering.*

Buying Young Shrubs

You can buy young shrubs as partially trained, container-grown plants from a garden center, or as balled-and-burlapped or bare-root plants from a nursery. You can also propagate your own, using simple techniques like cuttings or layering, which gives you control over growing conditions and an opportunity to begin immediately to train a well-shaped specimen.

What to look for

Young plants should be vigorous and healthy, with no obvious signs of pests, diseases, or disorders caused by poor nutrition, such as leaf-yellowing. If grafted, check that the graft union is streamlined, so that scion and rootstock join smoothly and strongly, without a kink in the stem.

The root system must be large enough to support the top-growth (*see far right*) and should never be potbound, since this will affect absorption of nutrients, which can lead to stunted growth. Avoid plants that have been encouraged to flower heavily for sale, or deadhead them as soon as possible.

Shoot tips are healthy, with no sign of scorch or dieback

New foliage is abundant and vigorous

Stunted top growth

Bare, leggy stems

Older leaves are glossy and healthy

Dead growth

Congested root ball

Good specimen
This camellia has healthy growth, glossy, disease-free foliage and an attractive, well-balanced top growth that is supported by a substantial root system.

Poor specimen
This Prostanthera has been in its pot too long; its root ball is compacted, and the soil mix is exhausted, resulting in leggy growth and dead shoots at the base and center.

PRUNING ON PLANTING

A well-chosen, healthy plant needs no pruning on planting except perhaps to tip-prune soft shoots to promote a bushy habit, or to shorten overlong shoots by no more than one-third of their length for a more balanced outline. Remove weak growth or damaged shoots and shoot tips, along with unnecessary stakes and ties. Deadhead plants that have flowered, so that the plant uses energy for growth rather than seed formation. On balled-and-burlapped or bare-root plants, which must be planted when dormant, cut away cleanly any damaged roots. Container-grown plants, which may be planted at any time of year, seldom need root pruning except to shorten any damaged roots to clean, healthy tissue.

ROOT-TO-SHOOT RATIO

An unbalanced root-to-shoot ratio – top growth that is far too large for the root ball to sustain – is the primary cause of poor growth after planting. A container-grown plant that has outgrown its pot will establish more quickly if, on planting, its top growth is reduced, either by shortening all stems by half, resulting in a bushy habit, or by cutting them back to the base to encourage taller, more upright growth.

SMALL ROOT BALL

Deciduous cuttings (below, left and right)
Forsythia naturally forms a single stem (left).
To encourage a more bushy habit, cut back the growing tip (right).

Evergreen cutting (right)
Ceanothus and many other evergreens branch low down to form a balanced shape and seldom need pruning on planting.

UNPRUNED SINGLE STEM

PRUNED TO INDUCE BRANCHING

PRUNING UNNECESSARY

PRUNING SHRUBS

As YOUNG SHRUBS GROW, routine tasks, such as the removal of dead, diseased, or damaged wood, should be dealt with as needed. Once shrubs have had a growing season in which to establish and have then become dormant, formative pruning can start. The main aim here is to create a balanced shape and thus develop their ornamental features.

FORMATIVE PRUNING

Evergreens tend to develop a neat habit and well-spaced branches naturally, so little formative pruning is needed. If necessary, take off cold-damaged growth, badly positioned, or weak stems, then tip-prune overlong stems to balance the outline. Deciduous shrubs are much more likely to benefit from formative pruning. If a shrub is to be a permanent feature of some stature, especially if it flowers on second-year or older wood (*see below, right*), it needs to develop with an open center to allow penetration of light and air. Remove any crowded or crossing stems or shorten them to strong buds or young shoots facing in the desired direction. Shrubs that flower on the current season's growth are cut back to a permanent woody framework every year. They are pruned hard from the outset to develop a base of strong stems (*see below, left*) to support vigorous annual growth. The framework is usually near ground level, but if extra height is needed, more moderate pruning will produce a taller framework.

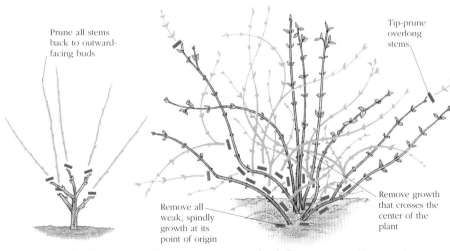

Prune all stems back to outward-facing buds

Tip-prune overlong stems

Remove all weak, spindly growth at its point of origin

Remove growth that crosses the center of the plant

Developing a low framework
Remove weak or badly placed shoots, then shorten strong remaining stems to healthy buds at the desired height.

Formative pruning, shrub flowering on older wood
Early pruning guarantees a well-shaped deciduous shrub with an uncluttered center at maturity. Remove unwanted stems while they are still small and while the plant is young and its healing potential is at its greatest.

ESTABLISHED DECIDUOUS SHRUBS

Shrubs that flower on new wood will bloom after midsummer and are pruned back to a permanent woody framework in early spring. During annual pruning, aim to restore a balanced framework and an open center. Remove dead or damaged wood as seen. Established deciduous shrubs that flower on second-year or older wood come into bloom before midsummer and are pruned immediately after flowering. Pruning cuts out some of the oldest wood each year, which encourages the production of young wood that flowers more freely.

Cut back flowered stems to nonflowered shoots

Cut out oldest flowered wood at its base

Deciduous shrub flowering on older wood
Prune directly after flowering to create an open center and a well-balanced framework of young, free-flowering wood.

ESTABLISHED EVERGREEN SHRUBS

Most evergreens need little pruning, but many tolerate harder pruning to remove wayward branches or to renovate them. Pruning removes diseased, damaged, or weak wood, thins out congestion, and removes badly placed stems. Deadheading helps the plant divert energy into growth rather than seed. Evergreens are usually pruned in spring, when danger of severe cold has passed. Flowering evergreens may also be pruned lightly after flowering, to remove the oldest flowered wood, to trim to shape, or, in areas with heavy snowfall, to thin dense growth on which snow could accumulate and cause breakage.

Cut flowered shoots to outward-facing buds

Pruning an established evergreen
Immediately after flowering, deadhead all flowering stems, cut away any damaged wood, and thin out congested areas.

ROUTINE TASKS

CHECK YOUR SHRUBS regularly and remove any diseased or damaged growth promptly before it becomes a problem. Other routine tasks include cutting out unwanted growth such as suckers, and deadheading. Where a shrub has become overgrown, hard pruning will give it a new lease on life.

REMOVING SUCKERS

The natural habit of many shrubs is suckering; sucker growth increases the plants spread and replaces stems that grow old and die. If the plant is congested, it is the oldest stems that should be removed.

On grafted shrubs, sucker growth emerges from below the graft union. This growth is usually stronger than the desirable grafted cultivar and must be removed if the suckers are not to predominate.

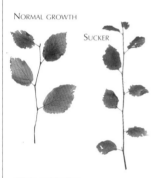

NORMAL GROWTH

SUCKER

Identifying suckers (left)
The shoot from a desirable Hamamelis mollis *cultivar (far left) is distinguishable from one arising from below the graft on the rootstock (left).*

Removing suckers (right)
Pull off sharply at the point of origin, either on the stem or root. If pieces remain, nip them off with a sharp knife without enlarging the wound.

DEADHEADING

Though not essential, deadheading improves the look of some shrubs, and more importantly, diverts energy from setting seed into further growth. Spent flowers are cut off with pruners, but for some shrubs, like rhododendrons, it is safer to pinch them out with finger and thumb.

Spent flower cluster

Non-flowered sideshoot

Pinching out (left)
Spent rhododendron flower heads are pinched out to avoid damage to new buds under the flowers (inset).

Cutting back (right)
On buddleias, use pruners to cut back a flowered cluster to a bud or young sideshoot.

REJUVENATION

If shrubs are neglected, they accumulate dead wood at their center and produce fewer flowers from congested old wood. Provided that the plants respond well to hard pruning and are basically healthy, pruning gives them a new lease on life. They are best rejuvenated in the dormant season, although sometimes this results in the loss of a season's flowers. Since all plants have a finite lifespan, even shrubs that respond well to hard pruning when young may not do so as they age. Propagate favorite plants as insurance against losses, and always feed and mulch well after pruning.

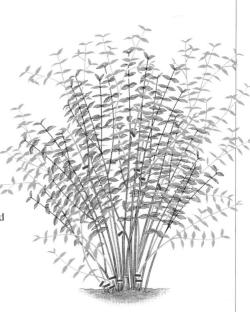

***Reinvigorating a shrub* (Philadelphus)**
Cut out dead, diseased, and crossing wood. Thin healthy shoots by half their number, to give the remainder room to develop.

DRASTIC RENOVATION

Several, mainly deciduous, shrubs respond well to drastic renovation when dormant. On vigorous plants, like the lilac (*Syringa*) shown here, this can be done in a single operation. If you fear that the shrub may not respond well, and many evergreens do not, renovate over two or three growing seasons. Take special care if renovating grafted plants not to cut below the graft union and to remove any regrowth that appears below it.

Reduce the weight of top growth before cutting back main stems

Cut back main stems to form a low framework

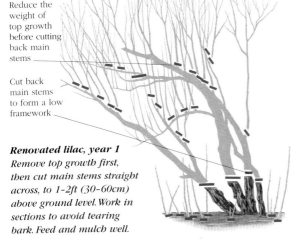

Renovated lilac, year 1
Remove top growth first, then cut main stems straight across, to 1-2ft (30-60cm) above ground level. Work in sections to avoid tearing bark. Feed and mulch well.

Renovated lilac, year 2
Many new shoots are produced in response to hard pruning. Thin these to 2-3 strong shoots per stump to form a strong framework.

SPECIAL EFFECTS

MOST SHRUBS ARE PRUNED using one or other of the techniques described on pages 58–61. A few, such as hydrangeas, have individual pruning requirements, while others respond well – and their ornamental features are maximized – if they are pruned specifically to achieve a particular shape, such as a weeping standard or a wall-trained shrub.

STAGGERED PRUNING

Coppicing and pollarding (*see pp.46–7*) are frequently practiced to produce vigorous young stems. In *Cornus alba*, *C. stolonifera*, and *Salix alba* cultivars young stems are brilliantly colored in winter in shades of scarlet, egg-yolk yellow, and lime green, an attraction that is dramatically enhanced when the shrubs are planted where the stems can be reflected in still water. A variation on the technique of coppicing, known as staggered pruning, takes this effect even farther. Cutting the stems of neighboring plants back to different heights results in successive bands of color, giving the impression of a sloping bank rather than a dense thicket of regrowth at a uniform height.

SHRUBS WITH CANELIKE STEMS

Some shrubs, for example *Kerria japonica* and *Leycesteria formosa*, flower on canelike stems produced annually from the base. The young canes add much to the overall effect, since they are beautifully colored in intense shades of green. Cut back one in three of the main stems immediately after flowering for *Kerria*, and in spring for *Leycesteria*.

KERRIA JAPONICA

Pruning at different heights (**Cornus alba**)
Let the shrubs grow unchecked for their first season. In late winter or early spring, cut back the stems of some plants to 2in (5cm), those of the next band to 10in (25cm), and the third to 20in (50cm).

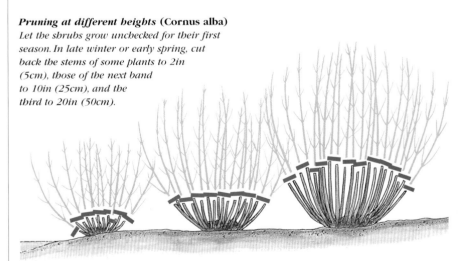

WEEPING STANDARDS

Many shrubs have arching or weeping branches, which are shown off well if the shrub is trained as a standard. The shrub you buy may have been pruned to make bushy growth (*see below, left*). Remove up to three-quarters of the top-growth, retaining a strong single stem furnished with laterals (see *below, right*). Train the single stem upright by tying it to a vertical stake. When it has reached the desired height, pinch out the leading shoot to encourage branching. Tip-prune new laterals as they develop to create a well-branched head. Keep the main stem clear of growth by rubbing out new laterals as they emerge or, if you miss them at this stage, pruning them flush with the trunk.

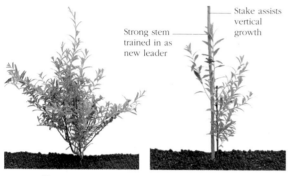

Strong stem trained in as new leader

Stake assists vertical growth

BEFORE PRUNING

AFTER PRUNING

Initial training (Buddleja)
Buddleja alternifolia *bears flowers on the previous year's wood and is pruned after flowering. Create a balanced shape and renew flowering wood by first removing old, weak, and unproductive growth. Cut back flowered stems to nonflowering young shoots, preferably those that are upward- and outward-growing, or to a strong bud.*

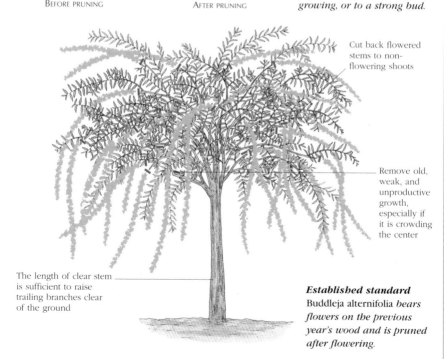

Cut back flowered stems to non-flowering shoots

Remove old, weak, and unproductive growth, especially if it is crowding the center

The length of clear stem is sufficient to raise trailing branches clear of the ground

Established standard
Buddleja alternifolia *bears flowers on the previous year's wood and is pruned after flowering.*

WALL TRAINING

Numerous shrubs can be wall trained in fans
or espaliers or less formally by tying in to
wires. Provide tough wire or trellis support.
Plant shrubs at least 18in (45cm) from
the base of the wall to avoid dry soil caused
by the "rainshadow" effect of the wall.
Cut single-stemmed plants back hard to
encourage branching, then select 4–5 strong
stems to form a well-spaced framework. Cut
inward- and outward-growing shoots back to
1–2 buds to induce sideways branching.

Initial training and pruning (Ceanothus)
If the shrub is well-furnished with laterals,
space them out and tie in to the support.
Shorten long laterals by a few buds to
produce branches for balanced coverage.

Shorten stems
that have
reached the
limits of the
allotted space

Deadhead flowered
growth and
shorten outward-
facing shoots

Check, reposition,
or replace any
broken or
constricting ties

Tie in new growth
and shorten weak
shoots to stimulate
stronger growth

Established shrub
As the shrub matures,
older, less productive
framework branches
may be removed to
make way for younger
growth. Continue to
tie in new growth and
reduce inward- or
outward-growing
shoots to 1–2 buds.

PRUNING PYRACANTHAS

Pyracanthas are grown for the clusters of small white flowers in early summer and for the showy, red, orange, or yellow fruits that follow them. They are borne on spurs – fruiting sideshoots – on the old wood.

Pruning to shape and the shortening of outward-growing shoots on wall-trained shrubs is done in midspring; to display the winter-persistent berries at their best, pruning can be repeated in late summer.

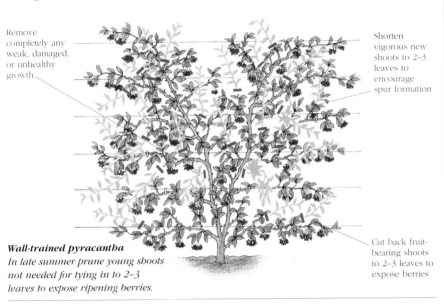

Remove completely any weak, damaged, or unhealthy growth

Shorten vigorous new shoots to 2–3 leaves to encourage spur formation

Cut back fruit-bearing shoots to 2–3 leaves to expose berries

Wall-trained pyracantha
In late summer prune young shoots not needed for tying in to 2–3 leaves to expose ripening berries.

PRUNING HYDRANGEAS

Hydrangea macrophylla and *H. serrata* bloom in late summer on the previous year's wood. In warm climates prune after flowering; in cool climates leave old flowers in place over winter to protect growth buds beneath them and prune in spring. Cut out weak shoots and 1–2 of the oldest stems at the base. Shorten the previous year's flowered branches back by up to 12in (30cm) to fat buds.

Pruning Hydrangea macrophylla
Prune in spring; if frost-damaged shoots are cut to the base they will regenerate freely but will not flower until their second summer.

Shorten flowered stems to a pair of healthy buds

PINCH-PRUNING

THE TECHNIQUE OF PINCH-PRUNING is used to induce bushy growth by repeatedly nipping out soft shoot tips using finger and thumb. It is suitable mainly for subshrubs, like fuchsias and coleus, which have woody bases and soft top-growth. Combine with training on wire frames or stakes and you can produce spectacular flower or foliage displays in many decorative shapes.

STYLISH SHAPES

With flowering plants, repeated pinching out delays flowering, because the shoot never has time to form a flower bud at its tip; its energy is diverted into forming sideshoots. If you cease pinching about two months before flowering, the last set of shoots, which all start into growth at the same time, will flower simultaneously. The striking result is well worth the time and patience taken to produce it.

Charm chrysanthemum
Grows naturally as a dense mound, so pinch-pruning to form a sphere is a relatively easy procedure.

Coleus standard
For fine foliage effects (right), pinch-prune to form a dense head on a clear-stemmed standard. This technique works well for coleus, Felicia, Pelargonium, Heliotropium, Abutilon × hybridum and A. megapotamicum.

Chrysanthemum sphere
Train three or four plants of cascade chrysanthemums (above) around a large wire balloon frame. Tie in growth to fill spaces and pinch out surplus shoots.

Argyranthemum cone
Most plants amenable to pinch-pruning can be formed into cones. Use three plants in a pot, as the more abundant growth makes it easier to pinch selectively to form a symmetrical shape.

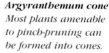

Fuchsia fan
Spread out and tie in fuchsia shoots to a stake framework arranged and tied as a fan; for extra support, attach a semicircle of wire netting to the frame before training.

PINCH-PRUNED STANDARD

Many subshrubs can be trained as standards, but coleus (*Solenostemon*) is one of the simplest. The height of the clear stem and head can vary according to the plant used and personal preference, but as a general rule the most pleasing results are produced if the depth of the head is one-third to one-half of the total height. The head's density is dictated by the frequency of pinching, the size of the leaves, and the distance between leaf joints. Coleus, with closely spaced leaves, is perfect for creating a dense "lollipop" head.

1 *Pot a single-stemmed cutting in a 10in (25cm) pot. Insert a stake and tie the stem to it. Feed well. Allow a week or so for the plant to settle in.*

2 *Until the desired height is reached, pinch out all sideshoots, but retain the leaves from whose axils they grew. This foliage nourishes the plant and helps thicken the stem. Tie in the stem at intervals with soft twine as it grows upward.*

3 *When the leading shoot reaches at least 8in (20cm) more than the desired height of the clear stem, pinch out the shoot tip.*

4 *At the head of the plant, pinch-prune all new shoots when they have two to four leaves, until a bushy head is formed. Pinch or rub out all shoots that appear on the stem.*

5 *Continue to pinch as necessary to keep a neat shape. On flowering plants, stop pinching 8–12 weeks before flowers are desired.*

Most leaves are shed naturally from the stem; if not, pick them off carefully.

SHRUBS IN CONTAINERS

ALL CONTAINER-GROWN SHRUBS need
more care than those in open
ground, since they have less
access to nutrients and water.
This is especially true of shrubs
that are pruned annually to
shape, as they rely on healthy, well-
fed foliage to keep them looking good.

Heliotropium *Viburnum tinus* *Nerium oleander*

Standards in pots
*Healthy, glossy foliage is essential for a fine-
looking standard; good nutrition is vital to
replace growth removed by pruning.*

ROOT PRUNING

When the roots of a mature shrub have
filled a large container it may not always
be feasible to repot it into a larger one –
or you may simply wish to keep it in a
favorite pot. The old soil mix will have
lost its structure and be depleted of
nutrients. In these circumstances, root
pruning is necessary. In spring, gently
slide the shrub from its container while
supporting the top-growth with one hand.

If the pot is full of roots, it may be necessary
to slide a long-bladed knife between soil mix
and pot to free the root ball. Remove surface
soil and loosen the roots with a hand fork to
relieve compaction. Prune back about a
quarter of nonfibrous roots by up to two-
thirds of their length, but retain the fibrous
roots. Repot using fresh soil mix, then prune
the shrub to reduce top-growth overall by
approximately one-third.

Teasing out roots
*Slide the plant gently from its pot (inset),
then gently tease out the roots with a hand
fork, shaking off as much old soil as possible.*

Pruning roots
*Shorten nonfibrous roots by up to two-thirds
of their length. Leave as many fibrous roots
intact as possible; these are the feeder roots.*

MAINTAINING NUTRITION

To sustain good healthy growth on a shrub that is pruned annually, the plant must have sufficient nutrients to replace the growth that is removed by pruning. Apply a balanced liquid fertilizer 2–3 times during the period between the start of growth in spring and midsummer. Until plants reach maturity, they should be repotted into a larger pot yearly or every other year in spring. When they reach their final pot size, root prune on repotting if necessary to relieve congestion *(see opposite, below)*. Otherwise, the top 2–4in (5–10cm) of soil mix can be removed and replaced with fresh soil mixed with a dressing of slow-release fertilizer at the manufacturer's recommended rate.

Demands of pruning and training

During the early years of creating, for example, this standard pyracantha, the demands on the plant's energy are great. It is vital therefore that some foliage is retained while the stem is being formed to allow the plant to manufacture the food it needs to grow and thrive.

Leader and laterals are continually shortened to create a bushy head

Laterals are shortened but retained to fuel the growth of a strong upright stem

Remove any strong sideshoots that would otherwise compete with the main stem

Pinch out any shoots on the clear stem. Leave single leaves to nourish the plant; they will be shed naturally as the plant matures

Bushy head is kept in shape by pruning after flowering; further material is removed in summer to reveal the fruits

Stem kept clear of growth

INITIAL TRAINING

TRAINING THE HEAD

ESTABLISHED PRUNING

INFORMAL BORDER PLANTS

A NUMBER OF SUBSHRUBS are commonly grown as informal border plants, as are bamboos and grasses. Subshrubs are generally smaller and more short-lived than other shrubs, with tender top-growth and a woody base, and produce their flowers on soft but vigorous annual growth. Some bamboos and grasses are evergreen, but others die down over winter.

PEROVSKIA

A subshrub with aromatic gray-green foliage, perovskia produces spikes of blue flowers on white stems in late summer. Top-growth dies back to a woody base in winter but is left in place to protect the new spring buds from frost and cold winds. In spring, prune flowered stems back to within 3–4 buds of the old wood, varying the height of each cut.

Pruning an established perovskia
In midspring, as new growth is breaking, prune flowered stems. Perovskia becomes leggy if left unpruned and loses stem color.

LAVENDER

Evergreen subshrubs, lavenders have aromatic, gray-green foliage and spikes of highly scented flowers in summer. They do not break freely, if at all, from old wood, so annual pruning is needed to keep plants compact and well-clothed with foliage. In warm climates they are pruned after flowering, but in colder climates autumn pruning is restricted to deadheading, leaving top-growth to protect next year's buds.

Autumn deadheading
In cold climates, deadhead in late summer or early autumn to keep the plant neat and to harvest the last of the flowers for drying.

Spring pruning
When danger of hard frosts has passed, cut back hard, removing most of the previous season's growth. Do not cut into old wood.

PAMPAS GRASS

Cortaderia selloana (Pampas grass) is a large, clump-forming grass grown for its spectacular flower plumes, borne in late summer. As the plant matures, the crown often becomes congested with dead foliage, which can crowd regrowth and reduce its vigor. Burning off top-growth used to be the routine advice, but this is risky; if the burn is not rapid and controlled, it simply destroys next year's growth buds. It is far safer to cut down the dead foliage and flower plumes as far as possible without damaging the new growth. This may be done in autumn in mild climates, but in colder regions, delay until spring. After cutting back, pluck out dried stem bases and leaves from the center of the clump. Always wear heavy gloves when handling pampas grass; the leaf margins are razor sharp.

Cutting back in spring
As new growth begins, use shears to cut the previous year's growth back as far as you can (inset) without damaging the new growth.

BAMBOOS

With the exception of some dwarf species, which can be clipped annually in early spring almost to ground level, bamboos require little pruning. Most need only the routine removal of broken, cold-damaged, or discolored canes in spring to keep them in good health. If a clump has become too dense, or if a species is grown for its attractively colored young stems, the canes can be thinned in spring or late summer.

Pruning canes
Wearing heavy gloves, use loppers to remove dead and damaged canes. Thin out the remaining canes by taking the oldest out at the base.

Clearing away
Without damaging the new shoots, clear away debris from the base to let in light and air and allow new canes to grow unchecked.

Restricting spread
Dig a trench deeper than the main root system around the desired margins of the clump, and insert a barrier of rigid plastic or slates.

ROSES

THE OBVIOUS APPEAL of roses lies in their exquisite flower forms and heavenly colors and scents. They are also enormously versatile, which has undoubtedly contributed to their popularity as a garden plant. Roses are extremely adaptable, tolerating a wide range of soil types, and there are types to suit almost every climate. When deciding how to prune a rose, the many cultivars, the range of recognized groups, and their varying requirements can seem daunting. Simply identify the manner in which a rose grows and flowers, and match it to a training program or pruning regime that best exploits its vigor, habit, and flowering performance, whether this is as a specimen plant, an informal hedge, or a cover for a variety of structures.

Rose arch *With its pliable stems, 'Climbing Iceberg' is suitable for training over an arch.*

TYPES AND FORMS

THERE ARE SOME 150 species of shrub and climbing roses, along with thousands of cultivars of hybrid origin. Because of their enormous diversity in size and habit, roses are extremely versatile, with plants to suit almost every garden situation. They are classified into several distinct types, each more suited to certain uses than others.

MAJOR GROUPS OF ROSES

Roses are divided into horticultural groups according to their growth habit, flower form, and flowering season, all of which have a bearing on their pruning needs. Cultivars are nearly always listed by category, which gives guidance as to their pruning requirements.

Modern bush roses

These include two major groups, the large-flowered bushes (hybrid teas) and cluster-flowered bushes (floribundas), as well as more recently developed miniatures, patio and polyantha bushes. These groups nearly all repeat flower.

Shrub roses

The shrub roses fall into three main groups: modern shrubs, which include groundcover roses, old garden roses, and the wild or species roses and simple hybrids of them.

Modern shrubs These are a diverse group of 20th-century origin and may flower once or repeatedly.

Old roses Among the most ancient of plants in cultivation, old garden roses are mainly European plants that pre-date the mid-19th century. Most flower once in midsummer.

Climbing and rambling roses

This group is made up of climbers, which usually flower repeatedly, and ramblers, which usually flower only once, around midsummer.

Shrub: old garden, upright habit
Medium-sized shrubs with upright growth and a dense habit. They need light pruning, with thinning and occasional removal of old stems to stimulate the growth of new, free-flowering shoots.

EXAMPLES
Rosa gallica var. *officinalis* and 'Versicolor', 'Belle de Crécy', 'Tuscany Superb', 'Charles de Mills', 'Duc de Guiche'.

Shrub: old garden, spreading habit
Spreading shrubs with thorny, arching stems. They are attractively informal, and pruning to restrict size spoils the habit. They need light annual pruning to remove some of the older, flowered wood.

EXAMPLES
Albas, ('Alba Maxima'), damasks ('Ispahan') mosses ('William Lobb'), centifolias ('Tour de Malakoff').

Shrub: modern

A "catch-all" group of diverse habit, size, and manner of flowering; includes groundcover roses. They do not need hard pruning.

EXAMPLES
'Buff Beauty', 'Penelope', 'Agnes', 'Fru Dagmar Hastrup', Jacqueline du Pré.

Modern bush: small

Miniatures are smaller hybrid teas and floribundas, usually no more than 10in (25cm) tall; patio and polyantha roses are closely related to floribundas. Their twiggy growth needs little pruning.

EXAMPLES
Anna Ford, Cider Cup, Pour Toi, Sexy Rexy, Top Marks, 'White Pet'.

Standard roses

Roses top-grafted onto clear stems of 20, 30, or 43in (50, 75, or 110cm) to form standards. The long-stemmed roses are used for weeping standards. They need pruning every year.

EXAMPLES
Many bush roses, patios, miniatures, polyanthas, groundcover roses, and weeping standards using ramblers and climbers.

Modern bush: hybrid tea and floribunda

These thorny shrubs of more or less upright habit flower repeatedly through summer on the current season's growth. They are pruned hard, removing most of the previous season's growth to stimulate new, free-flowering shoots.

EXAMPLES
Hybrid teas (large-flowered bushes), for example Peace, and Floribundas cluster-flowered bushes) such as Amber Queen.

Climbers

Thorny, long-stemmed, and of stiffly upright habit, these roses need support. They flower mainly on sideshoots from old wood and are pruned annually to stimulate more flowers.

EXAMPLES
'Aloha', Bantry Bay, 'Blairi No.2', Dublin Bay, 'Guinée', Handel, Leaping Salmon, 'Madame Hardy', 'New Dawn', Sympathie.

Ramblers

Often rampant grows, producing long, flexible stems from the base each year. Most ramblers bloom once, in summer. Entire flowered stems may be cut out after flowering.

EXAMPLES
'Albertine', 'American Pillar', 'Bleu Magenta', 'Emily Gray', 'Kiftsgate', 'Seagull', 'Treasure Trove'.

SELECTING ROSES

WITH SO MANY CULTIVARS to choose from, the selection of roses is largely a matter of taste; the difficulty arises if you have room for only one. The best way to discover your own preferences is to visit established rose gardens and note the habit, height and spread, fragrance, and color of roses that appeal to you.

WHAT TO LOOK FOR

Roses are sold with bare roots, for planting in the dormant season, or in containers, for planting at any time when weather and soil conditions are suitable. They should have healthy, well-balanced shoots, and if they are in leaf the foliage should be glossy, of good color, and free from obvious signs of pests, diseases, or disorders. Bare-root roses should have sturdy shoots and a good network of fibrous roots with no sign of damage or of having dried out. Standard roses should have a well-balanced head of strong shoots.

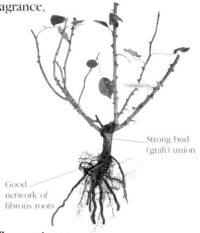

Strong bud
(graft) union

Good
network of
fibrous roots

Bare-root rose
Avoid buying plants with weak, spindly top growth, spindly, damaged or dried-out roots, or a stunted system of scant roots.

Sturdy, well-
balanced top-
growth

Moist soil mix
free of weeds
and moss

Vigorous
foliage of
good color

Container-grown rose
Do not buy plants with spindly shoots, sparse or yellow foliage, weeds in the pot, or signs of disease such as rust or blackspot.

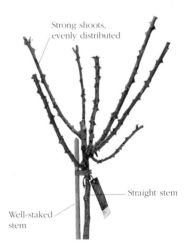

Strong shoots,
evenly distributed

Straight stem

Well-staked
stem

Standard rose
Avoid specimens with uneven top-growth or weak, crooked stems; the head should have strong, evenly spaced shoots.

BASIC TECHNIQUES

All roses have alternate buds. Make angled cuts just above buds facing in the direction in which you wish new shoots to grow. To maintain an open center, cut to outward-facing buds; on roses with arching shoots where inward- or upward-growing shoots are needed to fill the center, cut to an inward- or upward-facing bud. If no bud is visible, cut to the required height and trim back the stub when a dormant bud breaks.

| TOO RAGGED | BADLY ANGLED | TOO HIGH | JUST RIGHT | HEALTHY WOOD |

Good and bad cuts
A ragged cut allows ingress of diseases. Angling the cut wrongly allows water to collect near the bud, encouraging rotting. Leaving a long stub may result in dieback (see below); to remove, cut back into healthy wood. A correct cut gives the best chance of a strong shoot developing.

DEAD AND DAMAGED WOOD

The removal of dead, diseased, or damaged shoots is routine in the pruning of all roses. Crossing stems that rub are prone to damage and disease and should be shortened to a suitable bud or sideshoot. Make a clean, angled cut just above a bud facing in the required direction for a new shoot. With dead wood, cut to the demarcation line between live and dead wood to keep the "natural barrier" intact (*see p.17*). If shoots appear dried up and light brown, and no clear demarcation between dead and live wood can be seen, dieback is probably the cause; cut back to clean, healthy wood.

Dead wood

Crossing stems

New shoot

Dead stub

Routine pruning
Take out damaged and diseased stems and any that cross each other or the center of the bush. Cut out old unproductive wood completely. Remove any old stubs that have died back.

CUTTING TO A BUD

With a pair of clean, sharp pruners, angle the cut cleanly across the stem not more than ¼in (5mm) above a bud on the same stem or in a leaf axil. The cut should slope gently so that the lower end of it is directly opposite the bud.

CLEAN, ANGLED CUT

ROUTINE TASKS

TECHNIQUES TO ENCOURAGE more, or finer, blooms vary according to the particular rose group, but there are several routine operations apart from pruning out dead, damaged, or diseased wood that are applied to all roses. Regular deadheading, the removal of suckers, and the renovation of neglected plants are the basic requirements for healthy, vigorous roses.

DEADHEADING

A rose's energy is diverted into seed production if hips are allowed to develop. Roses that bloom once in summer are pruned after flowering, removing faded flowers in the process. Repeat-flowering roses are stimulated to produce a second or third crop of flowers by deadheading. Always cut to the second or third bud down the stem, with a full-sized leaf, rather than just nipping off the flowerheads.

Hybrid Tea Roses (left)
Cut to a strong, outward-facing bud or shoot below the faded flower to stimulate production of a new shoot.

Floribunda Roses (right)
Cut away the whole flowered truss when flowers have all faded, making a correctly angled cut just above a bud.

REMOVING ROSE SUCKERS

Many roses are grafted onto a wild rootstock, which may produce suckers that will weaken and eventually replace the cultivar if they are left in place. They usually occur at a short distance from the base of the rose and are identifiable because their leaves are a different shape and color. Cutting them off at ground level simply stimulates them into growth; they must be traced to their point of origin and carefully pulled off at the root.

Finding the source (left)
Scrape away the soil gently, and trace the sucker back to its point of origin.

Removing the sucker (right)
Pull the sucker sharply away from the root. This method is less likely to cause the sucker to regrow than cutting if off.

RENOVATING ROSES

Newly acquired gardens often contain badly neglected roses. Unless you replace or sterilize the soil, you cannot plant another rose in the same place because of the risk of replant disease. The dormant season is the best time to renovate, even for roses that are normally pruned after flowering, although you may lose a season's flowers. All renovation work should be followed by fertilizer and mulch in spring. Autumn is also the time to trim back tall roses, especially in exposed sites, to reduce wind-rock. The latter creates a gap in the soil, which may fill with water and freeze, damaging the graft union and ruining the plant.

BEFORE

AFTER

Autumn trimming to reduce wind-rock
Cut rose stems over 3ft (1m) tall back to a third or a half of their height in autumn so that winter winds do not damage the roots.

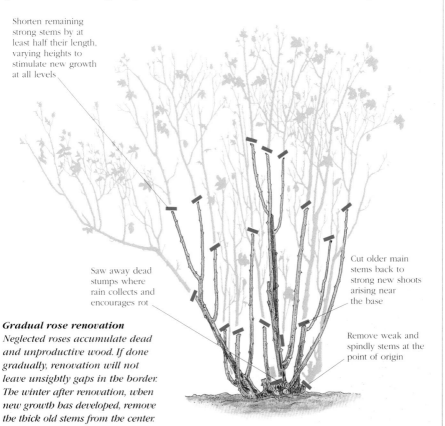

Shorten remaining strong stems by at least half their length, varying heights to stimulate new growth at all levels

Saw away dead stumps where rain collects and encourages rot

Cut older main stems back to strong new shoots arising near the base

Remove weak and spindly stems at the point of origin

Gradual rose renovation
Neglected roses accumulate dead and unproductive wood. If done gradually, renovation will not leave unsightly gaps in the border. The winter after renovation, when new growth has developed, remove the thick old stems from the center.

MODERN ROSES

THE AIM OF PRUNING all modern roses is to encourage plenty of new shoots that will bear a succession of flowers throughout the season. The two most important groups, hybrid tea roses and floribundas, are pruned back annually to a low framework of main stems. Other modern roses generally need less severe pruning to give their best.

BUSH ROSES

Hard prune modern bush roses immediately after planting to encourage growth from below. If you are planting a container-grown plant in the growing season, just remove open flowers and damaged growth, and prune hard next spring.

BEFORE PRUNING

AFTER PRUNING

Shoot tip is slightly damaged

Growth is already crossing and rubbing

Pruning a newly planted bush rose
Prune shoots to 3-6in (8-15cm) above
ground level, cutting to outward-facing
buds to form an open-centered bush.

HYBRID TEA ROSES

On established bushes, remove any dead or damaged growth as seen during the growing season, and deadhead regularly. During the dormant season (in cold climates delay work until early spring), the main pruning consists of removing unproductive and unhealthy shoots and shortening what remains. Make angled cuts to outward-facing buds to avoid crossing stems. The harder the pruning, the fewer, but finer, are the next season's flowers.

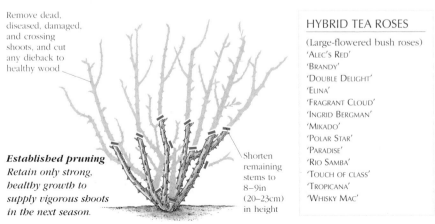

Remove dead, diseased, damaged, and crossing shoots, and cut any dieback to healthy wood

Established pruning
Retain only strong,
healthy growth to
supply vigorous shoots
in the next season.

Shorten remaining stems to 8–9in (20–23cm) in height

HYBRID TEA ROSES

(Large-flowered bush roses)
'ALEC'S RED'
'BRANDY'
'DOUBLE DELIGHT'
'ELINA'
'FRAGRANT CLOUD'
'INGRID BERGMAN'
'MIKADO'
'POLAR STAR'
'PARADISE'
'RIO SAMBA'
'TOUCH OF CLASS'
'TROPICANA'
'WHISKY MAC'

FLORIBUNDA ROSES

Once hybrid tea and floribunda roses are established the major pruning difference between them is that the floribundas are not pruned so hard. The charm of these roses lies in the mass of flowers clustered in one head, so more buds are retained on a longer length of stem in order that they may develop into flowering shoots. On shoots that have carried large trusses of flowers there may appear to be no buds to cut to, in which case just cut to the approximate desired height. This should stimulate a dormant bud into growth, and if a stub is left above, it can be cut away.

FLORIBUNDA ROSES

(Cluster-flowered roses)
'AMBER QUEEN'
'ANGEL FACE'
'APRICOT NECTAR'
'CHERISH'
'CLASS ACT'
'GRUSS AM AACHEN'
'ICEBERG'
'MATADOR'
'PLEASURE'
'SUNFLARE'
'SUNSPRITE'
'TANGO'

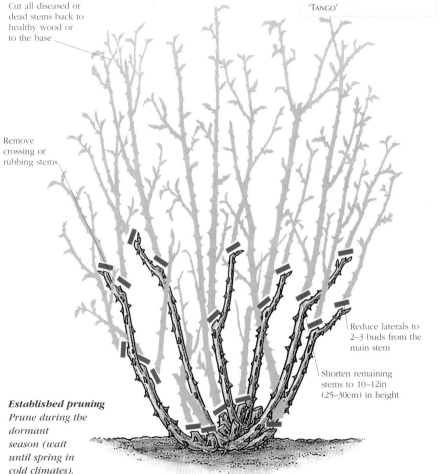

Cut all diseased or dead stems back to healthy wood or to the base

Remove crossing or rubbing stems

Reduce laterals to 2–3 buds from the main stem

Shorten remaining stems to 10–12in (25–30cm) in height

Established pruning
Prune during the dormant season (wait until spring in cold climates).

MINIATURE BUSH ROSES

These tiny bush roses are scaled down versions of hybrid tea or floribunda roses, and the principles of pruning are the same as for their larger counterparts - deadheading when flowering, and pruning when dormant. Prune hard on planting, cutting back to 2–3in (5–8cm) above ground level. Once established, and if growing well, again prune hard as shown. If growth is poor or in need of renovation, prune lightly, retaining and shortening only the strongest stems, as for larger bushes.

POPULAR EXAMPLES

ANGELA RIPPON
'ARIZONA SUNSET'
BABY MASQUERADE
DARLING FLAME
'EASTER MORNING'
MINNIE PEARL
PARTY GIRL
PEACHES 'N' CREAM
POUR TOI
'STACEY SUE'
STARINA
'SWEET FAIRY'
TEENY WEENY

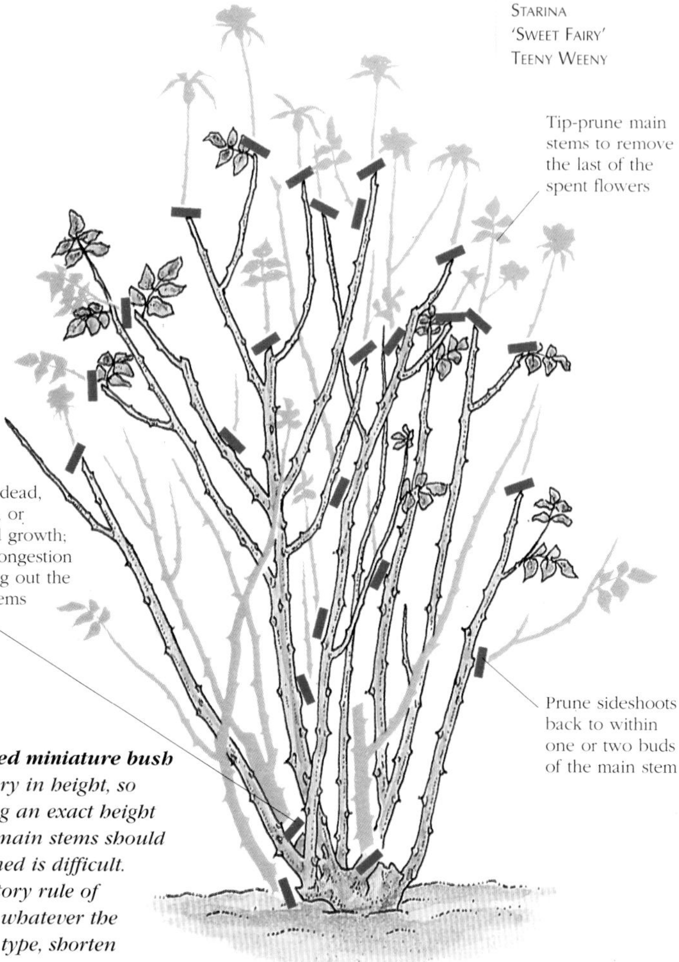

Tip-prune main stems to remove the last of the spent flowers

Remove dead, diseased, or damaged growth; relieve congestion by cutting out the oldest stems entirely

Prune sideshoots back to within one or two buds of the main stem

Established miniature bush
Bushes vary in height, so prescribing an exact height to which main stems should be shortened is difficult. A satisfactory rule of thumb is, whatever the flowering type, shorten main stems by two-thirds.

MODERN SHRUB ROSES

Many modern shrubs combine the vigor of a species rose with the repeat-flowering virtues of modern roses. They are pruned when dormant, in early spring. A few have a single flush of flowers and are pruned after flowering. Most shrub roses are bushy and vigorous, reaching heights of 4–6ft (1.2–2m), and need only light pruning *(see below)*. Some are tall cultivars of floribundas and are pruned in a similar way *(see p. 81)*, shortening main stems by only one-third to maintain stature. For the repeat-flowering hybrid musks, shorten strong stems by up to one-third and sideshoots by one-half. For rugosas, prune when dormant, tipping back long stems and occasionally taking out an old stem completely.

Supporting modern shrub roses
Two low stakes with strong twine form a useful support for the stems of open shrub roses and can be disguised by underplanting.

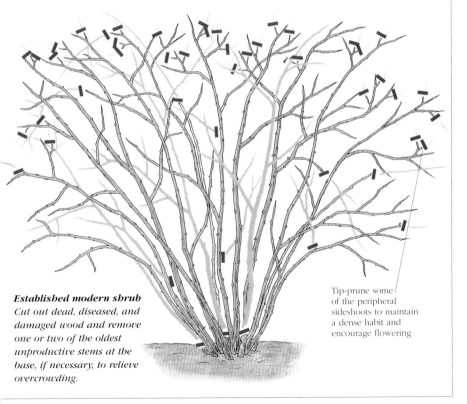

Established modern shrub
Cut out dead, diseased, and damaged wood and remove one or two of the oldest unproductive stems at the base, if necessary, to relieve overcrowding.

Tip-prune some of the peripheral sideshoots to maintain a dense habit and encourage flowering

GROUNDCOVER ROSES

There are two types of groundcover roses: the modern shrubs and the creeping ramblers. Both are pruned mainly to confine their spread. Modern shrub types have a spreading habit, and seldom exceed 2ft (60cm) in height. Prune repeat-flowering cultivars in spring, the rest after flowering, in summer. Cut out any dead or diseased stems and tip-prune main stems or shorten if overlong. Shorten laterals to keep an open center. Rambler types (*see right*) are pruned after flowering. Cut overlong stems back to upright shoots to keep them within bounds.

Vigorous first-year stems can be pegged down

Rambler-type groundcover rose
The vigorous rambler type of groundcover rose has long stems that will root into the ground, increasing the rose's spread.

STANDARD ROSES

A standard rose is created by top-grafting a selected rose onto a clear stem (heights may vary), which needs permanent staking. Standards are pruned according to the type of rose that forms the head, with the graft point being treated as if it were at ground level. The aim is to maintain a balanced head, free of crossing shoots and dead, diseased, or damaged wood. In areas with hard winters, autumn trimming is advisable to reduce the risk of strong winds damaging the head. Once-flowering roses are pruned after flowering; repeat-flowering types when dormant.

POPULAR EXAMPLES

HYBRID TEA ROSES:
'BRANDY', 'FRAGRANT CLOUD', 'LOVE', 'PEACE', 'SECRET'
FLORIBUNDA ROSES:
'AMBER QUEEN', 'ICEBERG', 'MATADOR'
PATIO, MINIATURE, AND POLYANTHA
'ARIZONA SUNSET', 'CHINA DOLL', 'STARINA', 'TOP MARKS'

Remove dead, damaged, and diseased growth

Pruning in early spring
Prune stems that were reduced in autumn to remove oldest wood, create a balanced head, and promote vigorous new flowering shoots.

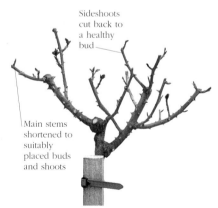

Sideshoots cut back to a healthy bud

Main stems shortened to suitably placed buds and shoots

After pruning
On remaining healthy main stems cut back to 8in (20cm) from the graft union, and shorten their sideshoots to 2–3 buds.

WEEPING STANDARDS

A weeping standard rose is produced by top-grafting a
rambler, climber, or trailing groundcover rose onto a clear
stem about 5–6ft (1.5–2m) tall. It is best left unpruned on
planting and for the first two years to develop its form.
Prune only to remove dead, diseased, and damaged wood,
or to shorten weak shoots to a strong bud. The more rigid
stems of climbers should be trained downward by tying to
a wire "umbrella" frame while still young. Once established,
prune according to rose type: rambler (*see p.88*), climber
(*see pp.88–9*), or groundcover rose (*see opposite*).

Pruning a rambler weeping standard
*After flowering, prune to remove oldest
flowered shoots and reduce sideshoots.
Shorten shoots that touch the ground.*

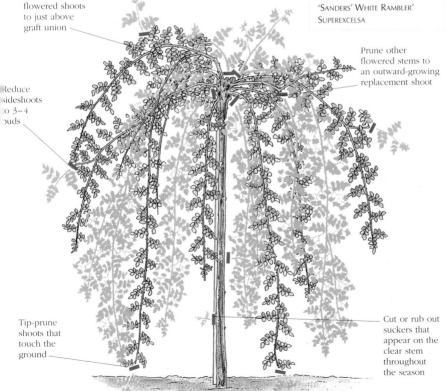

Cut back oldest
flowered shoots
to just above
graft union

Reduce
sideshoots
to 3–4
buds

Prune other
flowered stems to
an outward-growing
replacement shoot

Tip-prune
shoots that
touch the
ground

Cut or rub out
suckers that
appear on the
clear stem
throughout
the season

OLD ROSES

THE OLD GARDEN SHRUB ROSES are usually pruned in one of the two ways
illustrated here, depending on whether their habit of growth is dense and
upright, or more open and spreading. The majority flower in one glorious
summer flush and are pruned as soon as this is over; those that are repeat-
flowering are pruned the same way but in the dormant season.

UPRIGHT HABIT

Forming dense shrubs, gallicas are typical
of this group and bear fragrant flowers in
midsummer. Prune lightly on planting by
tipping back overlong stems and taking
out one or two stems if growth is crowded.
Once established, remove dead and

damaged growth in spring. After flowering,
thin growth out by shortening laterals back
to a main stem. Every one to three years,
remove one or two main stems at the base.
Gallicas make good informal hedges; clip
hedges lightly when dormant.

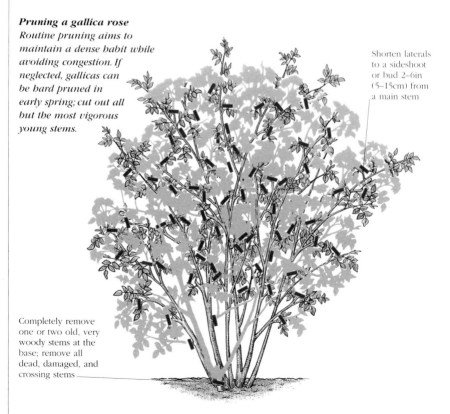

Pruning a gallica rose
*Routine pruning aims to
maintain a dense habit while
avoiding congestion. If
neglected, gallicas can
be hard pruned in
early spring; cut out all
but the most vigorous
young stems.*

Shorten laterals
to a sideshoot
or bud 2–6in
(5–15cm) from
a main stem

Completely remove
one or two old, very
woody stems at the
base; remove all
dead, damaged, and
crossing stems

SPREADING HABIT

This rose group is distinguished by the long, gracefully arching stems typified by alba roses, which flower once in midsummer. On planting, lightly tip back long shoots. Once established, prune after flowering to remove dead, diseased, and damaged wood, and thin crossing shoots. Cut back laterals and main shoots by one-third of their length. In autumn, shorten any very long, whippy shoots by up to a third to avoid damage by winter winds.

Pruning an alba rose
Routine pruning aims to relieve congestion and renew flowering shoots. Neglected shrubs can be cut back hard; remove all but the strongest young shoots, then shorten them by one-third.

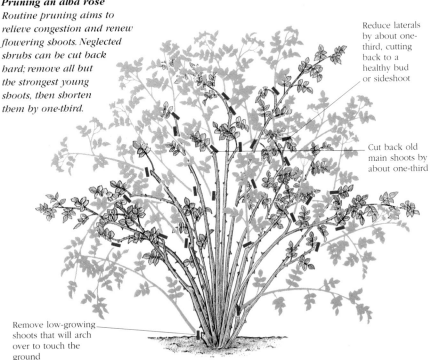

Reduce laterals by about one-third, cutting back to a healthy bud or sideshoot

Cut back old main shoots by about one-third

Remove low-growing shoots that will arch over to touch the ground

OLD GARDEN ROSES

UPRIGHT	SPREADING	CHINA	'HENRI MARTIN'
GALLICA	**ALBA**	'CÉCILE BRUNNER'	'NUITS DE YOUNG'
'ALAIN BLANCHARD'	'ALBA MAXIMA'	'HERMOSA'	'WILLIAM LOBB'
'BELLE DE CRÉCY'	'ALBA SEMIPLENA'	'MUTABILIS'	**PORTLAND**
'CHARLES DE MILLS'	'BELLE AMOUR'	'PERLE D'OR'	'COMTE DE CHAMBORD'
'COMPLICATA'	'CÉLESTE'	**DAMASK**	'MARCHESA BOCCELLA'
'DUC DE GUICHE'	'GREAT MAIDEN'S BLUSH'	'ISPAHAN'	'PORTLANDICA'
R. GALLICA 'OFFICINALIS'	**BOURBON**	'MADAME HARDY'	**PROVENCE ROSES**
'PRÉSIDENT DE SÈZE'	'BOULE DE NEIGE'	'OMAR KHAYYÁM'	'DE MEAUX'
'TRICOLORE DE FLANDRE'	'LOUISE ODIER'	**MOSS**	'FANTIN-LATOUR'
'TUSCANY SUPERB'	'MADAME ISAAC PEREIRE'	'CAPITAINE JOHN INGRAM'	'THE BISHOP'
'VIOLACEA'	'VARIEGATA DI BOLOGNA'	'CRISTATA'	'TOUR DE MALAKOFF'

CLIMBERS AND RAMBLERS

As THEY DIFFER in their mode of growth, climbers and ramblers have slightly
different pruning needs. Ramblers tend to produce long, flexible stems
annually from the base, with a single flush of flowers in summer. Climbers
have stiffer, more upright growth and usually produce a succession of
flowers from sideshoots that arise from a permanent woody framework.

WALL-TRAINED CLIMBERS

Climbers are sold with longer shoots than
those of shrub roses. These are not pruned,
since this would remove the buds needed
to produce plenty of new shoots. (It is very
important not to prune climbing sports of
shrub roses, since this makes them produce
nonclimbing growth.) Once growth begins,
if the main stems are slow to branch, prune
stem tips back to the first strong bud (make
this an outward-facing bud on outer stems).
This encourages sideshoots to develop.
Fan out the main stems, space them evenly,
and tie them in as nearly horizontal as
possible. Cover the lowest supports well
while young stems are still flexible; it is
difficult to fill any gaps lower down later
on. No further pruning is needed until the
framework is established, except to remove
dead, diseased, or spindly growth.

Tip-prune non-
branching main
stems by 2–3in
(5–8cm)

Planting and training
*Plant climbers 18in (45cm) away from the
base of the wall. Remove only dead, damaged,
or spindly growth. Tie in stems as they grow.*

WALL-TRAINED RAMBLERS

Ramblers produce their single flush of flowers most freely
on one-year-old shoots and readily make new growth at the
base each year. Plant 18in (45cm) away from the support.
Remove weak, spindly shoots. Cut main stems back to
healthy buds, 16in (40cm) above ground level, and train
shoots horizontally.

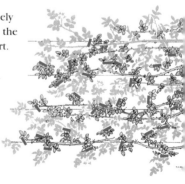

Established wall-trained rambler
*When plants fill their allotted space, thin and shorten excess
growth after flowering. Then cut out one in three of the main
stems at the base to ensure continued new growth. Remove
stems in sections to avoid damaging remaining shoots.*

ESTABLISHED CLIMBERS

Once a framework is established and fills its allotted space, pruning aims to confine spread and guarantee production of new flowering wood. Overlong shoots can be shortened at any time; cut them back to a strong bud. After flowering, cut back flowered sideshoots by two-thirds of their length to stimulate growth of next year's flowering shoots. As main shoots become less productive, after about three years, cut them back to their base or to a lower new shoot. Tie in all new growth and remove any dead, diseased, or weak shoots.

POPULAR EXAMPLES

'ALOHA'
ALTISSIMO
COMPASSION
DORTMUND
DUBLIN BAY
'NEW DAWN'
'PARADE'
'PINK PERPÉTUÉ'
SYMPATHIE
WHITE COCKADE
'WILLIAM ALLEN RICHARDSON'

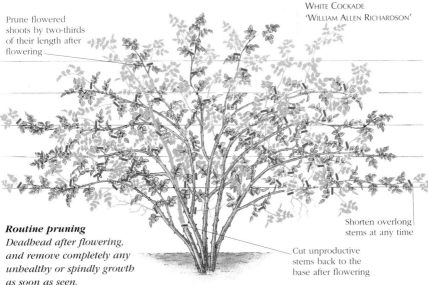

Prune flowered shoots by two-thirds of their length after flowering

Routine pruning
Deadhead after flowering, and remove completely any unhealthy or spindly growth as soon as seen.

Shorten overlong stems at any time

Cut unproductive stems back to the base after flowering

RESTRICTED RAMBLERS

Most ramblers are vigorous and too large for small gardens. The following are more restrained.
'ALBÉRIC BARBIER'
'ALBERTINE'
'CRIMSON SHOWER'
'FÉLICITÉ PERPÉTUE'
'GOLDFINCH'
LITTLE RAMBLER
'PAUL TRANSON'
'SANDERS' WHITE RAMBLER'
'VEILCHENBLAU'

Special Training

One of the major strengths of roses as a group is that they are amenable to training in so many attractive ways. They can be grown, for example, along ropes to create graceful swags, up vertical structures such as obelisks and tripods, and over pergolas, or they can simply be encouraged to scramble through trees or other suitable host plants.

Swags

Training a rambler or a climber with pliable stems on thick rope suspended between pillars makes attractive swags. Posts 7–8ft (2.1–2.5m) tall produce the best effect at eye level; make the rope 4–5ft (1.2–1.5m) longer than the distance between posts so that it dips about 2ft (60cm) midway. Plant roses 1ft (30cm) from the base of each post. Allow them to reach the post top before training and tying into the rope with garden twine.

1 In the first few years, prune according to the rose type. When the rose begins to crowd the rope, as here, more extensive pruning is needed to avoid spoiling the line of the swag.

2 Wearing heavy gloves, carefully detach the rose stems from the rope and unwind them until each main stem with its sideshoots can be distinguished from its neighbors.

3 Prune each of the flowered stems back to a vigorous shoot, creating an L-shape in the direction of growth; sideshoots that follow the direction of the rope will be easier to tie in.

4 Taking care not to damage the junction between main stem and sideshoots, lift the L-shaped stems up to the rope and wind young stems around it, attaching with garden twine.

PYRAMIDS AND TRIPODS

Roses suited to this form of training are the less vigorous climbers and any flexible-stemmed shrub roses. To cover the structure as quickly as possible, plant a rose at the base of each leg, about 10in (25cm) from the support, and splay out the stems around it. No initial pruning is needed other than removal of dead, damaged, or spindly wood. As growth proceeds, tie in the young pliable stems in evenly spaced spirals around the structure, as close to the horizontal as possible to encourage flowering laterals. Prune established roses as for climbers (*see pp.88–9*) or shrub roses (*see p.83*).

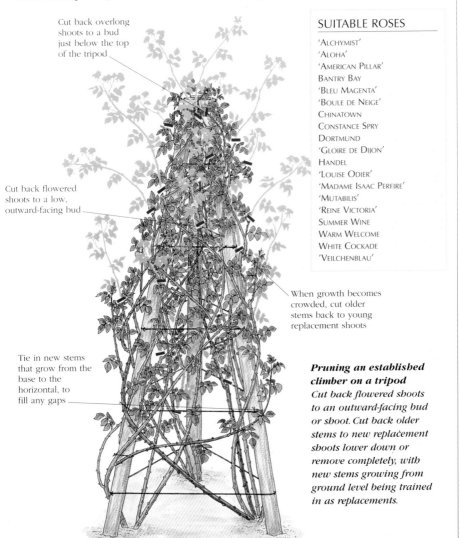

Cut back overlong shoots to a bud just below the top of the tripod

Cut back flowered shoots to a low, outward-facing bud

Tie in new stems that grow from the base to the horizontal, to fill any gaps

When growth becomes crowded, cut older stems back to young replacement shoots

SUITABLE ROSES

'ALCHYMIST'
'ALOHA'
'AMERICAN PILLAR'
BANTRY BAY
'BLEU MAGENTA'
'BOULE DE NEIGE'
CHINATOWN
CONSTANCE SPRY
DORTMUND
'GLOIRE DE DIJON'
HANDEL
'LOUISE ODIER'
'MADAME ISAAC PEREIRE'
'MUTABILIS'
'REINE VICTORIA'
SUMMER WINE
WARM WELCOME
WHITE COCKADE
'VEILCHENBLAU'

Pruning an established climber on a tripod
Cut back flowered shoots to an outward-facing bud or shoot. Cut back older stems to new replacement shoots lower down or remove completely, with new stems growing from ground level being trained in as replacements.

PILLARS AND PERGOLAS

Ramblers are obvious choices for large pergolas; for rustic pole structures or pergolas less than 6ft (2m) in length, climbing roses are more suitable. Plant the rose 10in (25cm) away from the base of the pillar; prune as for ramblers (*see p.88*), or climbers (*see p.88*). Train straight up the pillar, tying in shoots as they grow to wires or struts attached slightly away from the pillar's surface. Remove sideshoots to induce vertical growth. As the rose reaches the top of the pillar, tie in stems horizontally along the crossbeams; use additional wires or strips for support if you want to produce a "roof" of greenery. Vertical stems cease to flower well after 2–3 years; if flowers are desired on both top and pillar, plant a second, less vigorous rose and train it spirally as for a tripod (*see p. 91*).

Main stems will reach canopy more quickly if sideshoots are removed

Stems at periphery can be taken around and tied in to pillar sides

Training up a pergola pillar (right)
Avoid crossing and overcrowding as far as possible by spacing shoots evenly. Attach to wires or struts using figure-eight ties to avoid constriction or chafing.

Deadhead if practical; cut back to a low bud in a leaf axil

Tie in new shoots; staples make useful attachment points

On mature roses, cut out oldest stems at the base, teasing out in sections

FOR SMALL PERGOLAS

'ALBÉRIC BARBIER'
'BLUSH RAMBLER'
'CLIMBING CÉCILE BRÜNNER'
COMPASSION
'COMPLICATA'
'GOLDFINCH'
HIGH HOPES
LITTLE RAMBLER
'NEW DAWN'
'PHYLLIS BIDE'
'SANDERS' WHITE RAMBLER'
SYMPATHIE
'VEILCHENBLAU'
WHITE COCKADE

Pruning an established climber or rambler
Take great care when pruning from a ladder. Use guidelines for autumn pruning of ramblers (p. 88) and climbers (p. 88) but prune less hard.

TRAINING UP A HOST TREE

Ramblers and climbers are ideal for training up a host tree. Make sure that the tree is healthy and strong enough to bear the weight of the rose - a moderately vigorous climber would be suitable for a standard apple tree, while a rampant rambler needs a much larger woodland tree. Position the rose on the windward side of the host so that wayward shoots are blown into the tree. The shoots will make their way toward the sunnier side of the crown, so avoid a host on the sunny boundary of your garden if you want to fully appreciate the rose in flower. Plant the rose at least 4ft (1.2m) away from the tree base at the edge of the canopy, so that it is not robbed of moisture and nutrients by the tree. Twist or tie all the shoots to a heavy rope anchored to a peg in the ground and tied at the other end either to the tree's trunk or to a low branch. For the first two or three years it may be necessary to attach shoots of climbers to the lower branches of the tree. Most ramblers should climb unaided toward the upper branches.

Length of rubber hose threaded onto rope supporting rose protects branch fork

Formative training
Careful siting and initial training are needed to guide a rose to the lower branches; it will scramble up toward the light naturally.

PEGGING DOWN

Training rose stems horizontally to ground level by pegging down was a popular technique in Victorian times, especially for hybrid perpetual roses. Any rose with flexible shoots is suitable for this method. Allow a growing season to become established, then, after flowering, carefully bend stems to ground level and peg them down or tie them to wires. In following summers, deadhead repeat-flowering roses regularly. In autumn, cut out all weak growths and 2–3 older main stems; peg or tie down strong young stems as replacements. Shorten flowered laterals to 4–6in (10–15cm).

Shorten all upward-growing laterals

Trim back leading shoot to limit spread

Pegging down a hybrid perpetual
Trim back leading shoot on each pegged-down stem to confine growth. Shorten flowered laterals to 4–6in (10–15cm).

CLIMBING PLANTS

AN INFINITELY adaptable group of plants in terms of
garden design, climbers are indispensable when
providing height and backdrops for other plants.
They are also superb when grown in twining
associations to provide year-round displays and
combinations of foliage, flowers, and fruit. In the
wild, climbing plants concentrate their energies on
producing long, fast-growing shoots to scramble
over other plants and obstacles in their quest for
light. Pruning and training are vital when using
climbing displays in the garden, to shape, direct,
and sometimes restrict the plants' growth. Strong
supports are also essential – all climbers need
something to grow up, against, or through.

Wall-trained wisteria The vigorous and highly ornamental wisteria is ideal for house walls.

TYPES OF CLIMBING PLANTS

CLIMBING PLANTS have evolved a number of methods by which they support themselves on their upward quest for light. It is important to understand the way that they grow so you can provide appropriate support. Other aspects of growth, such as vigor and the ability to recover from pruning, also dictate the pruning and training methods needed.

CLIMBERS AND SUPPORTS

The way a plant climbs is not directly linked to its pruning needs but does affect its training. It is important to choose climbers whose growth habit suits their intended support. A wrought iron obelisk, for example, would be so rapidly swamped by rampant climbers like *Parthenocissus* or *Fallopia* (Russian vine) that the cost of such a decorative feature would be wasted. If a tree stump is to be masked, a dense-growing evergreen is more useful than a deciduous

climber that is bare in winter. It is equally important to choose methods of support that will enable a plant to climb or be trained successfully. An ivy will cling to and creep up a bare stone wall, whereas a honeysuckle needs guiding to wires or struts before it can twine around them. Winter jasmine, like other scramblers, will never make its own way up a vertical support unaided; each stem must be individually tied in to gain height and coverage.

Stem roots (Hedera)
Plants like ivy will cling to any rough surface by means of small, adhesive, aerial rootlets that arise from the stems.

Hooked thorns (Bougainvillea, above)
Many plants, like climbing roses, brambles, or bougainvillea (above), use sharp, sometimes hooked, thorns to anchor stems to their host.

Self-clinging climbers (Parthenocissus, left)
Parthenocissus *produces touch-activated adhesive pads, in the form of disklike suckers at the ends of tendrils. They adhere to any rough surface, like stone, brick, or tree bark.*

Twining stems (Wisteria)
Some stems will twine around any support they touch but may need initial guidance.

True tendril climbers (Passiflora racemosa)
Tendrils are twining shoots that grow out from the stem; they will twine around any thin support, then coil up and shorten to tighten their grip, often thickening to secure their hold.

Twining leafstalks (Clematis montana)
Leafstalks wind themselves around each other and any support that they meet; tying in is needed only to guide and direct growth.

Leaf tendrils (Cobaea scandens)
Modified leaves or parts of leaves form tendrils that reach out in search of support; such plants usually climb unaided rapidly.

FIXTURES AND FITTINGS

Twining and tendril climbers need wire, netting, or trellis to attach themselves to. Clinging climbers adhere unaided to wood, tree bark, or masonry. Scrambling plants like jasmine throw out long stems that climb over obstacles and need tying in to their support, whether trellis, laths, or wire. In nature, established stems that have died provide support for new basal shoots, but in gardens these are removed to reduce risk of disease.

VINE EYES (*INSET*) AND WIRES

Selecting a Climber

PERHAPS THE FIRST AND MOST IMPORTANT factor when choosing a climbing
plant is to check that its height and spread are suitable for its allocated
space. If you continually have to prune it hard to confine it within
bounds, you make an unnecessary amount of work for yourself and
are also unlikely to achieve the ornamental qualities, like flowers or
fruits, for which the plant is grown and valued.

Buying young climbers

Climbers are usually sold as container-grown
plants. The top-growth should be healthy
and undamaged, and free from any sign of
pests or diseases. Look for a well-balanced
framework of strong stems and fat, healthy
buds; avoid buying plants with weak spindly
growth and dead or damaged buds. Check
that the soil in the container is evenly moist,
and the surface is free of weeds and mosses
– their presence indicates that the plant may
have been in its container for some time and
may have suffered nutrient deficiencies.
The soil mix should be full of healthy living
roots, but the pots should not be so full that
the roots are coiled around in the pot or
protruding from the bottom.

Healthy green
foliage, free of
pests and diseases

Fat healthy buds
at the base of
strong stems

Soil mix
surface is free
of weeds and
mosses

Well-formed specimen
*The soil mix surface is free of weeds and
moss. The plant has strong, well-supported
stems with a complement of healthy new
leaves and fat buds at the base.*

Soil mix
evenly filled
with healthy,
pale-colored,
fibrous feeder
roots

Strong healthy roots
*The root ball is compact and the pale-colored,
healthy living roots fill the soil mix evenly.
There is no evidence of coiling, constriction,
or dead, brown roots.*

ROUTINE TASKS

Early training and, often, pruning is essential to encourage climbing plants to produce plenty of strong shoots that will grow to cover the available space (*see pp.100-101*). Some climbers from then on need only minimal attention, so select them for sites where access to the mature plant may be difficult, as in the branches of a tree, or high on a wall. Other climbers need pruning to remove dead and diseased wood, or to take out old growth, thus inducing replacement shoots or increasing flowering potential.

Deadheading may also be required. The amount of time spent cutting back overlarge plants can be minimized if the vigor of the plant is well matched to the site. Pruning to enhance flowering is often an annual or twice-yearly task, and timing is crucial. While neglected specimens of short-lived plants are best replaced, others can be rejuvenated by pruning. Those that respond well to hard pruning can be cut down nearly to ground level and new growth retrained to restore the feature to its original beauty.

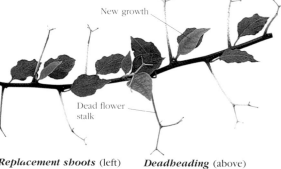

New growth

Dead flower stalk

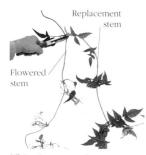

Replacement shoots (left)
Unless changing the direction of growth, prune to a shoot that follows the line of the older stem.

Deadheading (above)
If dead flowerheads or flower stalks are unsightly, pick or snip them off, taking care not to damage any new growth.

Replacement stem

Flowered stem

Thinning growth
Pruning for flowering usually involves removing flowered shoots. This is often enough also to prevent congestion.

Tracing stems
It may be hard to trace stems to the point of origin. Cut a stem at its base, then tease out wilted growth in sections.

Shearing dense climbers
Large, dense, and vigorous climbers can conveniently be cropped back to their supports with shears.

INITIAL TRAINING

MOST CLIMBING PLANTS are trained along walls and fences. Many of the same principles apply to the various types of training, even though plants may differ in their individual pruning needs. For permanent climbers, time and effort spent developing a good basic framework in the early years will be amply repaid as the plant matures.

ON PLANTING

Before planting, cut out any dead, damaged, or weak growth. If only one stem is needed, remove all but the strongest. If strong stems are few and more are needed, pinch out their tips to encourage branching near the base. However, if there is only one stem (as with many clematis), do not check its growth until after the first growing season. Then, in late winter or early spring, cut it back almost to ground level to promote new basal growth. If the climber is to be trained against a wall or fence, plant it 10–18in (25–45cm) away from the structure. Secure

young stems to the support, using twine tied in figure eights (*see opposite, below*). If necessary, use angled bamboo stakes to guide shoots to their support. Tie the shoots to the stakes and attach the stakes to the wires or trellis. Little or no pruning should be needed in the first growing season. As the climber grows, train shoots to the support in the desired direction (*see opposite*). Provided that the climber is not one that is cut down every year, the next few years should be spent developing a well-spaced framework.

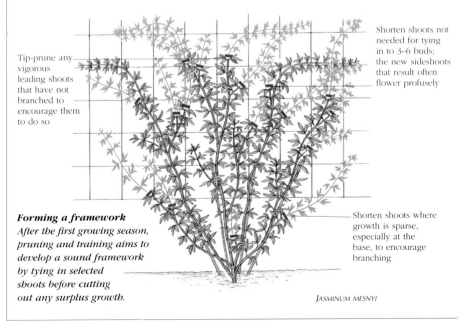

Tip-prune any vigorous leading shoots that have not branched to encourage them to do so

Shorten shoots not needed for tying in to 3–6 buds; the new sideshoots that result often flower profusely

Forming a framework
After the first growing season, pruning and training aims to develop a sound framework by tying in selected shoots before cutting out any surplus growth.

Shorten shoots where growth is sparse, especially at the base, to encourage branching

JASMINUM MESNYI

TRAINING IN STEMS

Guiding and tying in is crucial to obtain good coverage, particularly for wall-trained plants. Where the lower area of a support is to be covered, fan out some shoots from the start; gaps lower down are difficult to fill later on. This will encourage twining and tendriled plants to climb up the whole width of the allotted space, rather than straight up the middle. Always train some shoots horizontally to stimulate the production of flowers and fruit (*see p.13*). Cut back straggly shoots and any that grow in unwanted directions. Tie in as growth proceeds in order to cover the whole area.

INDOOR CLIMBERS

In cool climates, tropical climbers will thrive in a warm conservatory. Those plants with aerial roots need tying in to a sturdy moss pole, kept damp by misting, to provide support.

Aerial roots

Moss pole

EPIPREMNUM

Achieving good coverage
Untended climbers will always naturally grow upward rather than sideways and need careful initial training to make sure that the structure is covered evenly.

GUIDING AND TYING IN

Guiding in
Stems of twining and tendril plants must be guided into the support while still flexible.

Figure-eight ties
Twine tied like this allows for stem expansion and buffers stems against hard surfaces.

Neglected ties
Check and replace ties as necessary to avoid stem damage and constriction.

ESTABLISHED CLIMBERS

CLIMBERS TRAINED AS PERMANENT features against a wall or any other support need a certain amount of maintenance to keep them healthy and vigorous. Routine tasks can be done as soon as you see that they are necessary (*see p.99*), while the timing of pruning for shape and size depends upon the individual plant. Thinning and pruning old wood to induce the production of new shoots will also be needed as the plant matures.

MAINTENANCE PRUNING

Although the timing varies, maintenance pruning is generally best undertaken during the dormant season. When pruning to improve flowering, the age of flowering wood must be taken into account: plants that bloom on the previous season's wood usually do so before midsummer and are pruned after flowering, cutting back the flowered shoots to buds or new sideshoots

that will bear the next year's flowers. Those that flower on the current season's shoots are pruned when they are dormant, cutting sideshoots to 3–6 buds to create flowering spurs. Evergreens are often pruned in summer, as are vigorous climbers, when it becomes necessary to restrict growth. Beware of pruning too hard; it induces excessive growth with few flowers or fruit.

Pruning in the dormant season
Basic maintenance pruning keeps plants in good condition and encourages vigorous growth while restricting their spread.

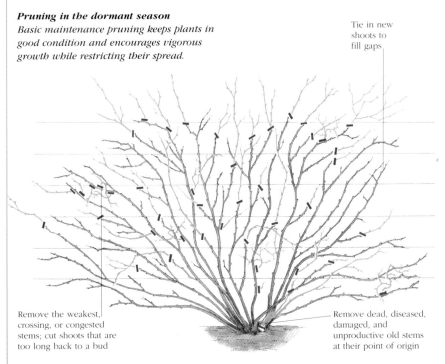

Tie in new shoots to fill gaps

Remove the weakest, crossing, or congested stems; cut shoots that are too long back to a bud

Remove dead, diseased, damaged, and unproductive old stems at their point of origin

RENOVATION

Neglected climbers soon become overgrown and revert to upward growth, which, when it becomes woody, is difficult to retrain. Dense, tangled growth may pull down supports and is likely to be full of dead wood, so that flowering and fruiting suffer. A plant that is moribund or suffering badly from pests and diseases is best replaced, but plants that are basically sound can be renovated in the dormant season. The easiest way is simply to cut the entire plant down, provided it will tolerate drastic pruning, and retrain the regrowth. If the plant will not tolerate drastic treatment or if you are unwilling to sacrifice the plant for the time needed for it to grow back, carry out stage pruning over 2–3 years.

Staged renovation
Over 2–3 years, cut back one in three of the main stems to ground level each year and tease out the severed top-growth.

TIMING OF PRUNING

AFTER FLOWERING
AKEBIA QUINATA
HYDRANGEA ANOMALA subsp. PETIOLARIS
JASMINUM NUDIFLORUM,
  J. OFFICINALE,
  J. POLYANTHUM
LONICERA PERICLYMENUM
SOLANUM CRISPUM

IN DORMANT SEASON
ACTINIDIA KOLOMICKTA
AMPELOPSIS
LONICERA JAPONICA
PARTHENOCISSUS HENRYANA,
  P. QUINQUEFOLIA,
  P. TRICUSPIDATA
VITIS COIGNETIAE,
  V. VINIFERA

Clear dead, diseased, and damaged wood from the plant, and remove any disease-harboring debris from behind the support

Use loppers to cut back one in three of the main stems to the base

Tie in strong new growth to fill gaps in the framework

SPECIAL TRAINING

A NUMBER OF CLIMBERS have pruning needs that differ slightly from the norm, and some can be pruned in several ways according to the structure you wish to achieve. Their versatility allows them to be grown through trees and shrubs, up walls and fences, over arches, pergolas, and wire supports, and even as groundcover with no support at all.

BOUGAINVILLEA ON PLANTING

Bougainvilleas are best displayed and trained against a wall – plant in a warm conservatory in cooler regions. They flower on the current season's growth, from summer to autumn in cool climates, and over a longer season in the tropics. Prune in late winter or early spring before growth begins. A well-spaced branch framework is essential, so on planting cut back hard to stimulate strong growth from the base.

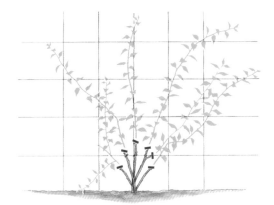

Pruning on planting, spring
Select 4-5 strong shoots and shorten them to 6-8in (15-20cm), cutting back to a bud facing in the required direction. Remove all weak and spindly shoots. As growth proceeds, tie in strong new shoots in a fan shape.

Year 2, spring
Prune the previous year's growth by three-quarters, then tie in new shoots as they appear. Cut sideshoots back to 2-3 leaves or buds so that flowering spurs will develop. Repeat annually until the allotted space is covered.

Established bougainvillea

Once the permanent framework has been established, the annual early spring pruning consists of tipping back any leading shoots that extend beyond the framework and shortening the previous season's sideshoots to 2–3 buds. This should leave spurs about ¾–1¼in (2–3cm) long, from which shoots will develop that will bear the current year's crop of flowers. During the growing season, remove weak, dead, and damaged growth as necessary. After flowering, deadhead by cutting back entire faded flower clusters to a young, nonflowering sideshoot. Old plants should respond to hard pruning but are better replaced.

BOUGAINVILLEA STANDARDS

B. glabra and *B.* × *buttiana* cultivars are good for training as pot-grown standards. Take a single-stemmed plant and secure it upright with a study stake. Shorten the leader on planting and clear the lowest laterals, leaving the rest as "trunk-builders." In the first winter, shorten the leader and cut laterals back to 2–3 buds. In summer, pinch out the leader at the desired height and shorten laterals by a third. Repeat winter pruning in the third year, and in summer remove laterals to create a clear trunk. Once a balanced head is formed, each year cut back all the previous season's laterals to within 2–3 buds of the branch framework.

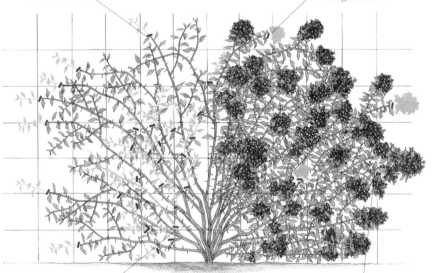

Where shoots exceed the allotted space, cut back to a healthy bud or sideshoot

Deadhead faded flowers, cutting the entire truss back to a young, non-flowering sideshoot

If growth is crowded, cut out some older stems and tie in a young sideshoot to fill any gaps

Maintenance pruning
Once a bougainvillea has reached the desired size, shorten overlong shoots and cut out crowded stems in early spring. In summer, deadhead faded flower trusses and tie in new shoots.

Tie in new shoots where there is space to do so

CLEMATIS

Prune clematis according to flowering season and the age of the wood that bears the flowers. The many species, cultivars, and hybrids fall into one of three groups. The initial pruning and training is the same for all groups. Provide sturdy support of wires or trellises and on planting, pinch out the young shoot tips. Tie in young stems to the support, taking care not to snap them.

Group 1 This group includes species and cultivars that flower early in the year on the previous season's wood. They are pruned immediately after flowering, although most need only minimal pruning once established.

Group 2 Comprises the large-flowered hybrids that flower early in summer on the previous year's wood and again later on the current season's growth. With careful pruning, the two periods virtually overlap, extending the flowering season. Prune in late winter or early spring before new growth begins.

Group 3 These clematis flower on the current season's growth in late summer. Prune in late winter or early spring, when buds show signs of growth.

CLEMATIS PRUNING GROUPS

GROUP 1 C. ALPINA , 'BLUE BIRD', C. CIRRHOSA, C. MACROPETALA, C. MONTANA and cultivars

GROUP 2 'BARBARA JACKMAN', 'BELLE OF WOKING', 'DUCHESS OF EDINBURGH', 'ELSA SPÄTH', 'HENRYI' , 'LASURSTERN', 'MARIE BOISSELOT', 'PROTEUS', 'THE PRESIDENT' , 'VYVYAN PENNELL'

GROUP 3 'ABUNDANCE', 'ETOILE VIOLETTE', 'GRAVETYE BEAUTY', C. ORIENTALIS, 'ROYAL VELOURS', C. TANGUTICA, C. VITICELLA

Thin dense growth, cutting back individual stems to healthy buds.

Group 1
Give minimal pruning, immediately after flowering; cut back overlong shoots to a healthy bud. Congested plants may be thinned.

Cut weak or damaged shoots to strong buds or to the base

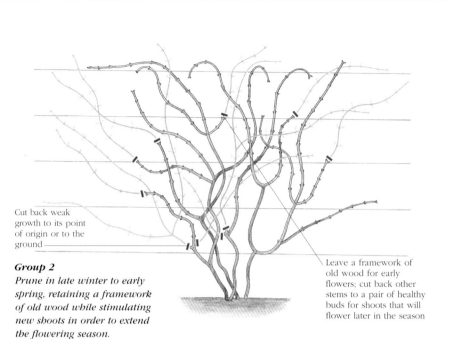

Cut back weak growth to its point of origin or to the ground

Group 2

Prune in late winter to early spring, retaining a framework of old wood while stimulating new shoots in order to extend the flowering season.

Leave a framework of old wood for early flowers; cut back other stems to a pair of healthy buds for shoots that will flower later in the season

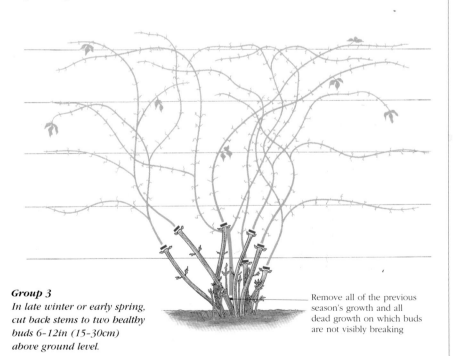

Group 3

In late winter or early spring, cut back stems to two healthy buds 6-12in (15-30cm) above ground level.

Remove all of the previous season's growth and all dead growth on which buds are not visibly breaking

WINTER JASMINE

A deciduous scrambling shrub, winter jasmine (*Jasminum nudiflorum*) bears primrose-yellow flowers on bare branches in winter and early spring on the previous summer's shoots. It does not cling and always needs tying in to its support if wall-grown, but left untied it will cascade to great effect over a bank or terrace wall. In either case, annual pruning is advisable; otherwise new growth simply scrambles over old, dead wood, which builds up messily, and creates a haven for pests and diseases. Winter jasmine is pruned in early spring, immediately after flowering. On planting, cut back young shoots by up to two-thirds of their length to encourage strong growth from the base. To wall train, tie in the resulting shoots evenly across the support to create a framework of branches. In subsequent seasons, continue tying in shoots as necessary to extend or fill the framework, and cut back flowered shoots to within 2–3 buds of the main branches, leaving the framework intact.

Building a framework
*Cut back hard on planting to encourage the production of new shoots. Tie in new shoots evenly across the framework to achieve good even coverage.
Remove dead, damaged, weak, and crossing stems altogether.*

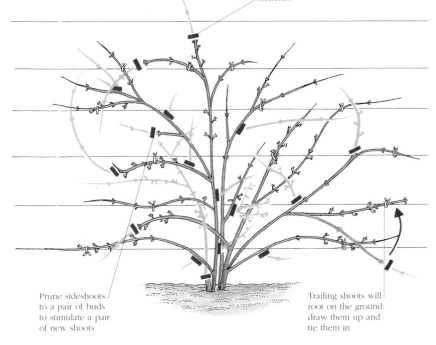

Prune vigorous unbranched stems to a pair of buds to encourage side branches

Prune sideshoots to a pair of buds to stimulate a pair of new shoots

Trailing shoots will root on the ground; draw them up and tie them in

CONTAINER-GROWN JASMINE

Jasminum polyanthum will tolerate the lightest of frosts if wall trained, but in cool climates it is more often grown as a house or conservatory plant, much valued for its intensely fragrant white flowers.

These are borne from late spring to early summer on the previous year's shoots and grow well if the plant is trained to a wire hoop or on trellises. *J. polyanthum* is pruned immediately after flowering.

1 Jasminum polyanthum *remains quite small when confined to a pot, but it quickly becomes congested and is best pruned annually.*

2 *Detach the plant carefully from its support and gently untangle the stems, spreading them out around the pot. Check that the support is still sound, and replace it if necessary. Repot or top-dress by carefully scraping away a shallow layer of soil and replacing it with fresh soil mix.*

3 *Prune all the long flowered shoots by cutting them back to nonflowering sideshoots or to a pair of strong, healthy buds.*

4 *Carefully retrain the plant over the frame, guiding the stems to the best effect and gently tying them in as evenly as possible around it.*

5 *Feed the plant to obtain vigorous new shoots. Guide these horizontally around the frame to stimulate flowering sideshoots.*

WISTERIA

In late spring and summer wisterias bear their drooping clusters of beautiful pealike flowers on lateral spurs arising from old wood. Most are rampant climbers that can take seven years or more to begin flowering, and on very rich soils they tend to produce an excess of leaf growth at the expense of blooms. As mature wood always flowers the most profusely, they benefit from the additional warmth that they receive when grown on a sunny wall. They are amenable to training in a number of ways, but the espalier form is perhaps the most perfect for displaying the hanging chains of flowers at their best. To maintain trained forms and enhance flowering, wisterias must be rigorously spur-pruned in two stages: in summer, about two months after flowering, and in midwinter.

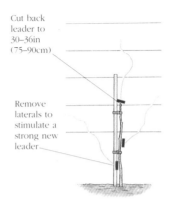

Cut back leader to 30–36in (75–90cm)

Remove laterals to stimulate a strong new leader

Pruning on planting
Cut back the leader to a strong bud about 30-36in (75-90cm) above ground level, taking care not to cut below the graft union on grafted cultivars. Remove all laterals.

Leave the leader unpruned and tie in vertically

Year 1, summer
Tie in the leader vertically, then select two strong laterals and tie them in at 45° angles. Prune any sideshoots to about 6in (15cm) long or to 3-4 buds to begin the formation of flowering spurs.

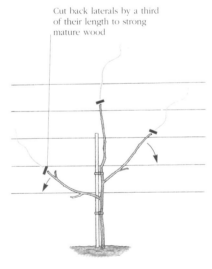

Cut back laterals by a third of their length to strong mature wood

Year 2, winter
Cut back the leading shoot to about 30in (75cm) above the topmost laterals. Lower the pair of laterals that were horizontally trained to 45° angles, and tie them to the lowest wires. Cut back by a third of their length.

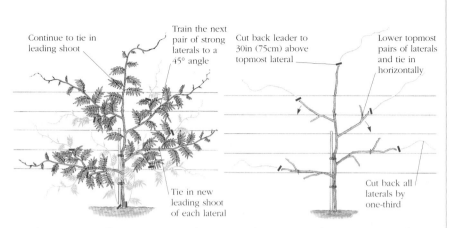

Continue to tie in leading shoot

Train the next pair of strong laterals to a 45° angle

Tie in new leading shoot of each lateral

Cut back leader to 30in (75cm) above topmost lateral

Lower topmost pairs of laterals and tie in horizontally

Cut back all laterals by one-third

Year 2, summer, until space is covered
Tie in the leading shoot and lowest laterals as they grow. Prune sideshoots arising from the laterals to 3-4 buds. Select the next pair of laterals and tie them in at 45° angles.

Year 3, winter, until space is covered
Shorten the leader to 30in (75cm) above the topmost pair of laterals; lower these horizontally and tie in; prune all laterals by a third of their length to strong mature wood.

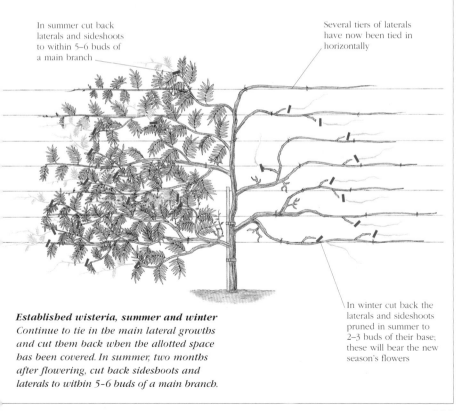

In summer cut back laterals and sideshoots to within 5–6 buds of a main branch

Several tiers of laterals have now been tied in horizontally

In winter cut back the laterals and sideshoots pruned in summer to 2–3 buds of their base; these will bear the new season's flowers

Established wisteria, summer and winter
Continue to tie in the main lateral growths and cut them back when the allotted space has been covered. In summer, two months after flowering, cut back sideshoots and laterals to within 5-6 buds of a main branch.

GRAPES

As rampant climbers, grapes (*Vitis vinifera*)
can be trained in a number of ways. In cool-
summer climates, cultivars are grown under
glass to guarantee a good crop. Pruning
is imperative to keep grapes under control
and fruiting well; where space is limited
the "rod-and-spur," or cordon, system (as
shown here) is the most suitable. Grapes
are borne on new wood arising from wood
made the previous year, so annual pruning
back to a permanent "rod," which may be
productive for decades, is required. For
good-quality fruit, do not allow the plant
to fruit at least until at least its third year; it
must become fully established if it is to bear
increasingly heavy crops. Thereafter, fruiting
is controlled by pruning and thinning to
produce fewer but finer bunches of grapes.
The main pruning is done in midwinter
when the risk of sap "bleeding" from cuts is
at a minimum, with some summer pinching
to control vigorous leaf growth.

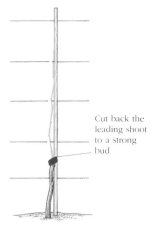

Cut back the
leading shoot
to a strong
bud

Rod-and-spur system: year 1, winter
*Plant vines in late autumn or early winter.
Before midwinter, cut back the leading shoot
by two-thirds to a strong bud on ripe wood
at or near the lowest wires; cut back harder
if the wood is unripe. Remove any laterals.*

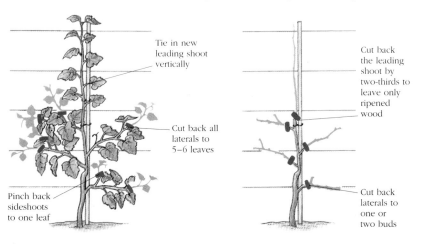

Tie in new
leading shoot
vertically

Cut back all
laterals to
5–6 leaves

Pinch back
sideshoots
to one leaf

Cut back
the leading
shoot by
two-thirds to
leave only
ripened
wood

Cut back
laterals to
one or
two buds

Year 1, summer
*Allow the leading shoot to grow unchecked,
and tie in vertically. Cut back each lateral to
5-6 leaves. Pinch or cut back to one leaf any
sideshoots on the laterals, including any that
emerge after laterals have been shortened.*

Year 2, winter
*Cut back the leader by two-thirds of the
summer's growth, or more if necessary, to
leave only ripe brown wood. Prune back
laterals to one bud if it looks strong, or
two if it doesn't appear so.*

Tie in the leader vertically as it grows

Cut back leader by half to two-thirds to leave only ripe brown wood

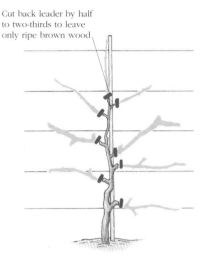

Year 2, summer
Tie in the new leading shoot vertically. Cut back each lateral to 5-6 leaves of the current season's growth. Pinch back to one leaf any sideshoots arising from the laterals. Remove any flower trusses that form.

Year 3, winter
Cut back the leader by a half to two-thirds, with the top bud facing the opposite way to the previous year's. Shorten laterals to one bud if it is strong, two if not. In spring, reduce new growth from each spur to two shoots.

Spring pruning allowed two shoots to grow at each spur; pinch out the weakest

Prune back laterals without flower trusses to 5–6 leaves

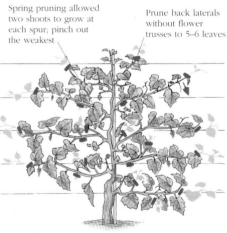

Lower the leader in midwinter and retie vertically when buds break in spring

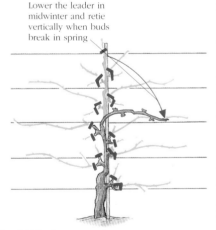

Established grape, summer
Prune laterals without flowers to 5-6 leaves, those with flowers to 2 leaves beyond the last truss. Pinch out trusses to one per lateral for table grapes, one every 12in (30cm) for wine. Pinch back sideshoots to one leaf.

Established grape, winter
Cut leader back to a bud below the top wire; tie it horizontally to encourage shoots to break low down. Prune laterals to one bud if strong, two if not. If spurs become congested, saw off the oldest section with a pruning saw.

VERTICAL FEATURES

Training climbers on arches, pyramids, and pergolas lends a strong vertical element to a design. Choose plants that will be capable of covering the structure without swamping it, and, if vigorous, will tolerate hard pruning to restrict their size. Some, such as *Cobaea scandens*, can be trained close to a support, while others, such as honeysuckle, develop into a cascading feature. Where winter appearance is immaterial, herbaceous climbers, such as *Canarina,* or those which tolerate severe pruning and produce vigorous basal stems that will reach the height of the structure in one season (for example, *Clematis viticella*) are the easiest to manage. For more permanent features, spiral flexible stems around the structure for the first 2–3 years to produce a well-spaced and free-flowering framework. The support should be well furnished with wires, netting, or trellises.

Training climbers on an arch
Fit the arch with plastic netting to provide attachment for climbing stems. Trim back overlong shoots to maintain shape and keep the pathway through the arch clear.

Long shoots are spur-pruned / annually to within 2–3 buds of main stems

***Pergola-trained* Passiflora**
Plants such as Passiflora *that flower on spurs are ideal for a pergola; the main shoot is trained horizontally and flowering sideshoots hang from wires. Clothe bare pillars with annuals, roses, or small shrubs.*

MIXED PLANTING EFFECTS

When mixing two or more plants together, choose combinations that will prolong the season of interest or provide contrasts of color or form. Site the plants on different sides of an arch, and train them so that their stems entwine; on a wigwam structure, grow different plants up each leg of the support (*see below*). In the latter case, a vigorous climber can be planted centrally and trained vertically so that it cascades from the top to meet the plants that have been trained up the sides. It is all too easy to cut the wrong stems when pruning intertwined plants, so select plants with similar or complementary pruning needs; for example, train a permanent woody-stemmed, spring-pruned climber up one side of a support and cover the other with rapidly growing herbaceous or annual climbers.

GOOD COMPANIONS

ASARINA with a white-flowered ROSA or CLEMATIS
JASMINUM POLYANTHUM with HOYA CARNOSA
LONICERA PERICLYMENUM 'BELGICA' with CLEMATIS 'JACKMANII' or C. 'POLISH SPIRIT'
RHODOCHITON with HUMULUS LUPULUS 'AUREUS'
VITIS VINIFERA 'PURPUREA' with annuals such as LATHYRUS ODORATA or TROPAEOLUM MAJUS
WISTERIA SINENSIS with a pink rose such as 'NEW DAWN'

TRIPOD PLANTED WITH MIXED CLIMBERS

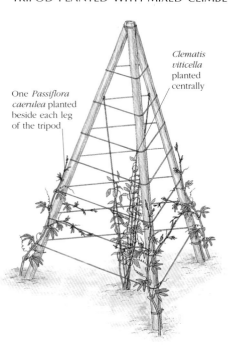

Clematis viticella planted centrally

Prune all trailing sideshoots of passion flower back to within two buds of horizontal stems

One *Passiflora caerulea* planted beside each leg of the tripod

Clematis with Passiflora, training
Train and tie in the lateral shoots of Passiflora to make permanent horizontal arms along the wires. The clematis climbs unaided.

Pruning, early spring
Cut back trailing sideshoots of Passiflora to two buds from main stems first, then prune clematis to 6in (15cm) above ground.

FRUIT TREES

THE DESIRE FOR full-flavored fruit that has not been treated with chemicals has stimulated a revival of interest in the traditional skills and pleasures of fruit-growing. Many cultivars for the garden have both ornamental and cropping potential, a bonus that helps justify their pruning and training demands on the gardener. Pruning and training play a major role in fruit-tree cultivation; all fruit tree forms need careful shaping and regular maintenance pruning to maximize yields of high-quality fruit. The introduction of dwarfing rootstocks that produce small, compact, and easily managed trees has brought fruit-tree cultivation within reach of those with even relatively small plots – extensive orchards are no longer necessary to enjoy fully the fruits of your labors.

Apple espalier *Decorative and productive, an espalier needs systematic pruning and training.*

Fruit Tree Forms

ALTHOUGH MOST FRUIT TREES can be trained into almost any shape, several distinct forms have been developed that are sympathetic to the growth habits of the individual trees and suit various garden situations and sizes. All fruit trees – in whatever form you choose – need careful pruning and training if they are to be both ornamental and maintain high-quality yields.

Selecting suitable shapes

When choosing a fruit tree form, there are three main factors to consider. Growth habit is the first. If you want to grow an apple tree against a wall, the espalier form is ideal, because it suits the way most apples fruit – on short sideshoots, known as spurs. Second, consider the space available. Many fruit trees cannot pollinate themselves and must be grown with compatible pollinating partners to secure a crop. If space is limited, several cordons can be sited in the same space needed by just one fan or bush. Third, take into account how much time and attention you are prepared to devote to your trees. Free-growing forms, like a bush or half-standard, are relatively easy to shape and maintain, needing one annual pruning in winter. More elaborate forms, like an espalier or cordon, need precise training in their early years and a pruning plan that may stretch over several weeks in summer. Even when established, these are high-maintenance specimens.

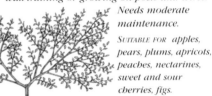

Fan
A decorative heavy cropping form, ideal for wall-training or growing on posts and wires. Needs moderate maintenance.

SUITABLE FOR *apples, pears, plums, apricots, peaches, nectarines, sweet and sour cherries, figs.*

Espalier
Must have the firm support of a wall, fence, or strong posts and wires. Needs intensive training and high levels of maintenance, but very productive.

SUITABLE FOR *apples and pears. Most other fruits, especially stone fruits like peaches or plums, are unsuitable for training to this form.*

HOW ROOTSTOCKS AFFECT TREE SIZE

Fruit trees ("M" series for apple rootstocks shown here) are grafted onto rootstocks that vary in vigor, thus controlling, and often dwarfing, the tree's eventual size. Be sure the rootstock suits both site and desired form.

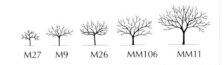

M27   M9   M26   MM106   MM11

Cordon

Ideal for growing several cultivars in a small space, and thus insuring good pollination. Excellent for good yields of high-quality fruit.

Moderately high maintenance.

SUITABLE FOR *apples that bear fruit on spurs (not those few that fruit at branch tips such as 'Lord Lambourne') and pears.*

Dwarf pyramid

Similar to the pyramid, but 5–6ft (1.5–2m) tall. Needs a dwarfing rootstock. Suitable for a hedge if planted 4–5ft (1.2–1.5m) apart. Pruning must be disciplined, but form is simple to train and maintain.

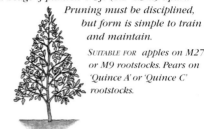

SUITABLE FOR *apples on M27 or M9 rootstocks. Pears on 'Quince A' or 'Quince C' rootstocks.*

Pyramid

The tapering form allows fruits on the lower branches to receive plenty of sun. A compact, easily maintained form, about 8ft (2.5m) tall, suitable for confined spaces.

SUITABLE FOR *ideally, plums grafted onto the rootstocks 'Pixy' or 'St Julien A', but will suit most plums except for strongly upright growers.*

Stepover

Essentially a modified cordon that is bent over at right angles and trained horizontally on strong posts and wires. An attractive form to use as low edging in a kitchen garden or bed.

SUITABLE FOR *spur-bearing, not tip-bearing, apples. Few other fruit woods are flexible enough to bend at right angles without breaking.*

Half-standard

A bush tree on a taller clear trunk, 4½ft (1.3m) high, and suitable for a large garden. Ideal form if growing for ornament and cropping. Needs a vigorous rootstock. Its height can make pruning and harvesting difficult.

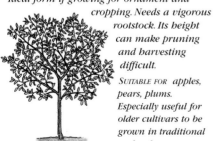

SUITABLE FOR *apples, pears, plums. Especially useful for older cultivars to be grown in traditional orchards.*

Bush

The most widely used form for a large variety of tree fruits. Structurally strong, productive, and fairly easy to train and maintain. Although quite short (grown on a clear trunk up to 3ft/90cm tall), it spreads widely so needs considerable space. Available on a wide range of rootstocks.

SUITABLE FOR *apples, pears, quince, plums, sour cherries.*

SELECTING FRUIT TREES

ALWAYS BUY FRUIT TREES from specialty fruit nurseries. They supply strong, healthy, well-trained stock and will give you reliable advice on the suitability of your intended site and whether the particular tree you want is self-pollinating or needs another cultivar nearby in order to set fruit.

BUYING YOUNG TREES

Specialty nurseries often sell young trees on which early form-training has already been done. The alternative is to buy one- or two-year-old trees to train yourself. In either case, use the same criteria when choosing a fruit tree as for selecting ornamental trees (*see p.30–1*), but check also on the vigor, position, and direction of growth of any laterals, since these are crucial to building up a strong branch framework.

Young untrained trees
In the first year, a tree will develop as a single stem or "whip" on which laterals may form (when it is known as a "feathered whip"). A two-year old feathered tree will have plenty of laterals from which to make a selection when forming a branch framework.

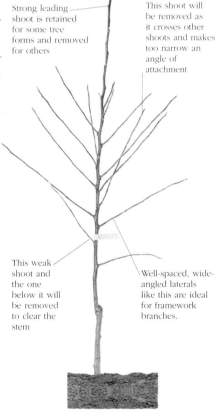

Single, strong shoot well-covered in healthy leaves

Straight, vertical stem

Graft point

ONE-YEAR-OLD WHIP

Strong leading shoot is retained for some tree forms and removed for others

This shoot will be removed as it crosses other shoots and makes too narrow an angle of attachment

This weak shoot and the one below it will be removed to clear the stem

Well-spaced, wide-angled laterals like this are ideal for framework branches.

TWO-YEAR-OLD FEATHERED WHIP

PARTS OF A FRUIT TREE

The pruning of fruit trees is one of the most skilled and well-understood of pruning techniques; it has, after all, been practiced for centuries. It is an art that has its own precise vocabulary for describing different parts of the fruit tree, and a little time spent familiarizing yourself with the most important terms will be rewarded by a better understanding of the techniques and consequently healthy and productive trees.

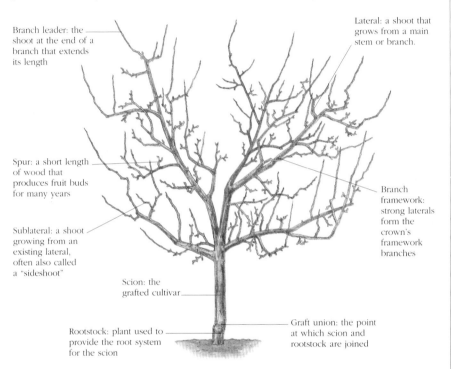

Branch leader: the shoot at the end of a branch that extends its length

Lateral: a shoot that grows from a main stem or branch.

Spur: a short length of wood that produces fruit buds for many years

Branch framework: strong laterals form the crown's framework branches

Sublateral: a shoot growing from an existing lateral, often also called a "sideshoot"

Scion: the grafted cultivar

Graft union: the point at which scion and rootstock are joined

Rootstock: plant used to provide the root system for the scion

BUDS AND FRUIT-BEARING GROWTH

A growth bud varies in appearance slightly, but is generally a narrow pointed bud that will develop into a new shoot or spur. A flower bud is fatter and more rounded than a growth bud, containing next season's flowers. The graft union is the point at which the scion (cultivar) is grafted onto the rootstock. It should be 4–12in (10–30cm) above soil level. A spur is a short-jointed shoot that bears fruit buds rather than growth buds, often for many years.

GROWTH BUD

FLOWER BUD (APPLE)

GRAFT UNION

SPUR

Basic Techniques

THERE ARE three main aims when pruning and training fruit trees: to influence the direction of shoot growth, ensuring structural strength and the desired shape; to protect the tree's health by prompt removal of dead, diseased, and damaged wood as well as crossing and crowded branches; and to maintain a good balance between cropping and growth. Every pruning cut you make should have at least one of these aims in mind.

Response to Pruning

The skill of fruit-tree management lies in using pruning and training to influence the balance between growth and the formation of flower buds. The pruning season is during winter dormancy, or in summer for stone fruits such as plums and peaches. To maintain the size and balanced shape of a mature tree, the most important rule is to prune weak shoots hard and stronger growth lightly. After hard pruning, the roots have fewer buds to feed, so these have good growth potential, resulting in strong new shoots but few flower buds. Little or no pruning leaves a smaller ration of nutrients per bud, yielding an abundance of small fruits at the expense of the young growth that would in time bear future crops. The nature of pruning depends on the state of the tree – whether it lacks strong new growth or is growing well but cropping lightly – and on where new growth is needed to replace old wood nearing the end of its useful life.

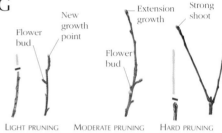

LIGHT PRUNING   MODERATE PRUNING   HARD PRUNING

Weak shoots
With light pruning, weak shoots form flower buds but do not grow much longer. With moderate pruning, growth and flower-bud development are both encouraged. With hard pruning, strong growth is formed at the expense of flower buds, but this may be necessary if replacement shoots are needed.

Strong shoots
Tip-pruned shoots produce extension growth and flower buds; moderate pruning increases branching and reduces flower buds; hard pruning gives strong growth at the expense of flower buds.

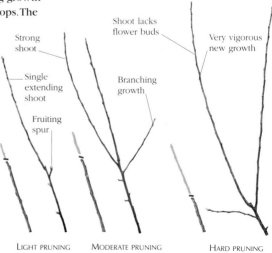

LIGHT PRUNING   MODERATE PRUNING   HARD PRUNING

MAKING CUTS

Narrow blade nearest the bud

Cutting to a bud (left)
Approach with the pruners from the opposite side to the bud to avoid damage from closing blades.

Replacing shoots (right)
Choose a strong shoot growing in a direction that enhances the tree's shape; cut in line with its growth.

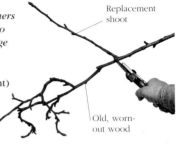

Replacement shoot

Old, worn-out wood

SPUR FORMATION

Long laterals

Pruning laterals
To stimulate formation of fruit buds near their bases, shorten long laterals to 5-6 buds, weaker ones to 2-3 (left); leave short laterals unpruned. Prune branch leaders by up to a third of their length, cutting to a bud (right). The fruits develop close to the main branches, reducing risk of breakage.

Branch leader

SPUR-THINNING

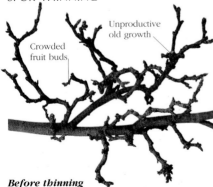

Unproductive old growth

Crowded fruit buds

Space between fruit buds will allow fruits to develop

Old spurs have been removed in favor of younger wood

Before thinning
After several years, spur systems become congested and overcrowded, leaving too little room for fruits to develop properly.

After thinning
Older, more complicated growth has been cut out, leaving younger wood where possible. Weak spurs have been removed completely.

SUMMER PRUNING

All formally trained tree forms are pruned in summer using the basic technique shown below to restrict growth and encourage fruit buds to form. It also discourages later, secondary growth, which may be vulnerable to cold damage. Pruning starts when the lower third of new shoots becomes woody and growth begins to slow, but precise timing depends on the weather. Shoots will become ready for pruning over a 2-3 week period.

TRAINED FRUIT TREE: SUMMER PRUNING

1 *Before pruning, new laterals have grown rapidly on this apple espalier, and are now ripening from the base. If not pruned, they can shade fruit from the ripening sun and rapidly outgrow their site. All new shoots 6–9in (15–23cm) long are shortened when the lowest third of the shoot has turned woody. New shoots emerge from the trunk and main branches, as well as from existing laterals and spurs.*

2 *Shorten new shoots* (left) *growing from the trunk and main branches to three leaves above the basal cluster.*

3 *Shorten sideshoots* (right) *from existing laterals or spurs to one bud above the basal cluster of leaves.*

4 *After pruning, good form is restored to the espalier branch, and more sun can reach the ripening fruits. Pruning cuts made in summer also stimulate the development of future flower buds. If any secondary growth does occur, prune shoots back to a bud at the base in midautumn to avoid frost or cold damage.*

GUARANTEEING A GOOD HARVEST

Blossom thinning
*If fruit trees bear only every
other year, remove 9 out
of 10 flower trusses a week
after flowering.*

Before fruit thinning
*If crowded fruits are all
allowed to mature, they will
be small and sour, and their
weight may break branches.*

After fruit thinning
*Excess fruits have been
removed to leave room for
the remainder to develop
to full size and sweetness.*

PREVENTING BRANCH BREAKAGE

*Young trees need a supporting stake, at least
until they are established. To keep branches
from breaking, loop them up with soft
twine tied to an extension stake that is
lashed to the vertical stake.*

A nail pounded into the
extension stake prevents
strings from slipping down

Support branches with soft
twine or ribbons of soft
plastic netting, which will
not damage bark

Keep branches clear
of the ground to
prevent fruit from
spoiling

APPLE BUSH

ONE OF THE MOST useful apple tree forms, the apple bush is also one of the easiest to train. A variety of rootstocks is available (*see p.118*), giving a wide range of heights in mature trees; to accommodate their spread even the smallest dwarf rootstocks must be planted at least 6ft (2m) apart.

FORMATIVE TRAINING

The aim is to create a branched, open-centered crown with 8-10 branches radiating from a short trunk, about 24-30in (60-75cm) tall. Start in winter with a feathered two-year-old tree that has three or four strong, wide-angled, and well-spaced laterals 2-3ft (60-90cm) from the ground. This form is also suitable for pears, plums, cherries, peaches, and nectarines, although these stone fruits are pruned in summer.

Training an apple bush form
Most apples are spur-bearers (see p.118); a few are tip-bearers, fruiting on longer shoots. Pruning differs according to fruiting habit.

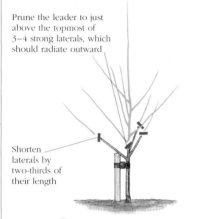

Prune the leader to just above the topmost of 3–4 strong laterals, which should radiate outward

Shorten laterals by two-thirds of their length

PRUNING ON PLANTING, WINTER

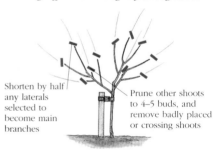

Shorten by half any laterals selected to become main branches

Prune other shoots to 4–5 buds, and remove badly placed or crossing shoots

YEAR 2, WINTER

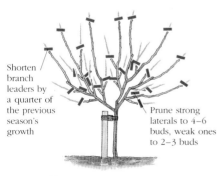

Shorten branch leaders by a quarter of the previous season's growth

Prune strong laterals to 4–6 buds, weak ones to 2–3 buds

YEAR 3, WINTER, FOR SPUR-BEARERS

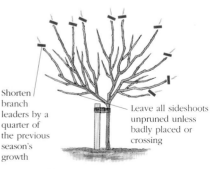

Shorten branch leaders by a quarter of the previous season's growth

Leave all sideshoots unpruned unless badly placed or crossing

YEAR 3, WINTER, FOR TIP-BEARERS

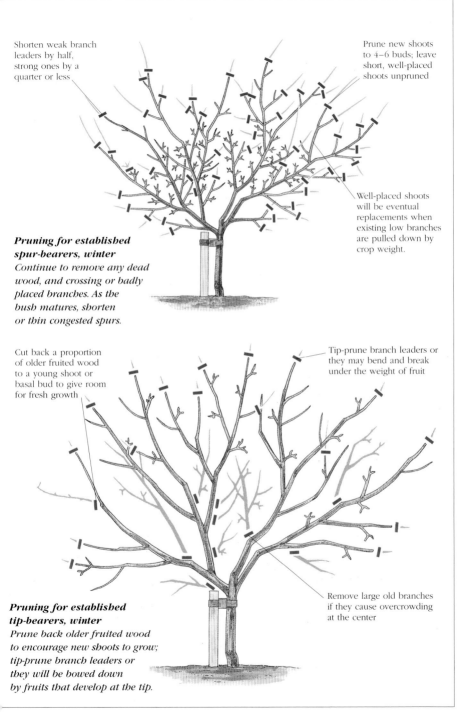

Shorten weak branch leaders by half, strong ones by a quarter or less

Prune new shoots to 4–6 buds; leave short, well-placed shoots unpruned

Well-placed shoots will be eventual replacements when existing low branches are pulled down by crop weight.

Pruning for established spur-bearers, winter
Continue to remove any dead wood, and crossing or badly placed branches. As the bush matures, shorten or thin congested spurs.

Cut back a proportion of older fruited wood to a young shoot or basal bud to give room for fresh growth

Tip-prune branch leaders or they may bend and break under the weight of fruit

Remove large old branches if they cause overcrowding at the center

Pruning for established tip-bearers, winter
Prune back older fruited wood to encourage new shoots to grow; tip-prune branch leaders or they will be bowed down by fruits that develop at the tip.

127

APPLE CORDON

A CORDON CONSISTS of a single main trunk along which the laterals are pruned in summer and winter to produce fruit-bearing spur systems. This style of pruning is suitable for spur-bearing cultivars only. Cordons are ideal for small gardens, since several pollination-compatible cultivars can be grown to yield substantial crops in a relatively restricted space.

TRAINING AND PRUNING

You can either buy ready-trained cordons from specialty suppliers or begin with a feathered whip or two-year-old tree with well-spaced laterals. Cordons need strong horizontal support in the form of a set of wires 24in (60cm) apart, stretched tautly between strong uprights 7½ft (2.2m) tall. These can be freestanding or fixed 4–6in (10–15cm) away from a wall or fence. Space individual plants 30in (75cm) apart; if a double row is required, space at 6ft (2m) apart. Plant at an angle of 40–45° to the ground, tying the stems to a bamboo stake lashed to the wires. Shorten long laterals to create fruiting spurs but do not cut the central leader until it reaches the top wire, when it should be pruned back to a weaker shoot in late spring.

CORDON FRUITS

All apples, except tip-bearers, can be grown as cordons. The technique is also suitable for pears. Cordons are often used to produce fruits for exhibition, as the technique combines maximum exposure to sunlight with all the vigor from a large root system directed into top-growth restricted by pruning.

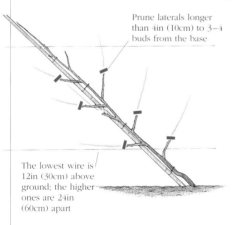

Prune laterals longer than 4in (10cm) to 3–4 buds from the base

The lowest wire is 12in (30cm) above ground; the higher ones are 24in (60cm) apart

Pruning on planting, winter (above)
Plant the tree at a 40–45° angle to the ground. Tie it to a 10ft (3m) long bamboo stake lashed to the wires. Leave the leader unpruned; shorten long laterals to 3–4 buds.

Year 1, summer (below)
As they ripen, prune new laterals from the main stem back to 3 leaves above the basal cluster; prune sideshoots from existing laterals to one leaf to initiate spur formation.

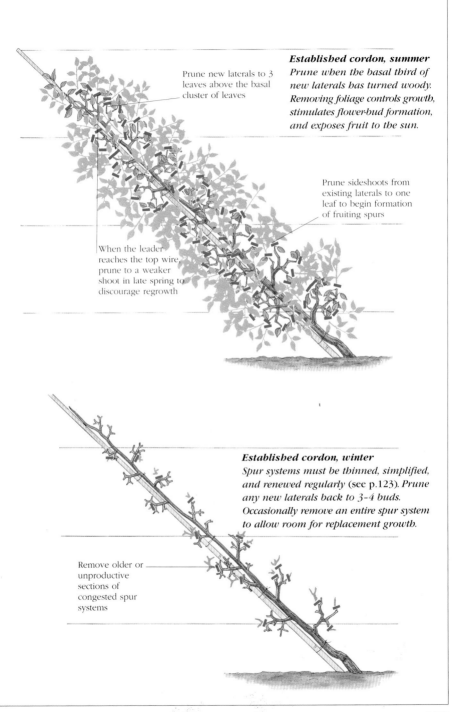

Prune new laterals to 3 leaves above the basal cluster of leaves

Established cordon, summer
Prune when the basal third of new laterals has turned woody. Removing foliage controls growth, stimulates flower-bud formation, and exposes fruit to the sun.

Prune sideshoots from existing laterals to one leaf to begin formation of fruiting spurs

When the leader reaches the top wire, prune to a weaker shoot in late spring to discourage regrowth

Established cordon, winter
Spur systems must be thinned, simplified, and renewed regularly (see p.123). Prune any new laterals back to 3-4 buds. Occasionally remove an entire spur system to allow room for replacement growth.

Remove older or unproductive sections of congested spur systems

APPLE ESPALIER

THE BEAUTY of the espalier form lies in its formal symmetry, so you should aim to produce pairs of branches of equal length as nearly opposite to each other as possible. An espalier's productivity results from the reducing effects of horizontal training on apical dominance. Espalier training is ideal for spur-bearing apples and pears, but unsuitable for stone

PRUNING AND TRAINING

Espaliers must have firm support in the form of a wall or strong fence with taut, horizontal wires set 18-24in (45-60cm) apart and 4-6in (10-15cm) clear of the wall. Two-tiered, freestanding espaliers can be used as fruit-bearing "fences" or dividing barriers. For three or more tiers, a vigorous rootstock is necessary. Precise early training is essential; this is easiest with a whip, but if you can find a feathered tree with one or two pairs of nearly opposing laterals you have a head start. Training is done in two stages, with the laterals first trained diagonally to keep them growing strongly, then lowered horizontally at the end of the growing season.

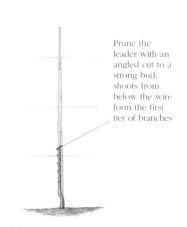

Prune the leader with an angled cut to a strong bud; shoots from below the wire form the first tier of branches

Year 1, winter
On planting, cut back the leader to a strong bud 2-3in (5-8cm) above the lowest wire. This bud will produce a new leading shoot.

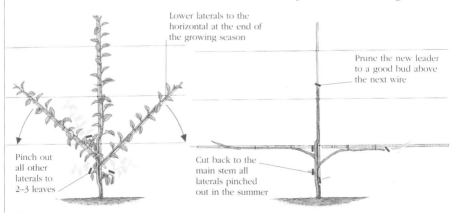

Lower laterals to the horizontal at the end of the growing season

Prune the new leader to a good bud above the next wire

Pinch out all other laterals to 2–3 leaves

Cut back to the main stem all laterals pinched out in the summer

Year 1, summer
Using stakes tied to the wires, train the leader vertically and two opposing strong laterals of equal vigor at a 40° angle to the ground.

Year 2, until all tiers are formed, winter
If growth is weak, prune laterals back by a quarter of their length. Remove all other laterals that were reduced in the first summer.

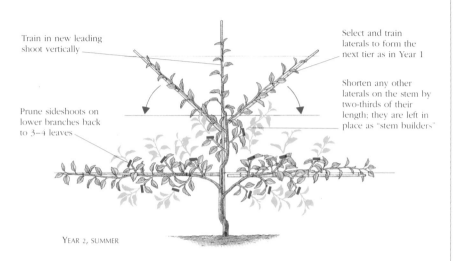

Train in new leading
shoot vertically

Select and train
laterals to form the
next tier as in Year 1

Shorten any other
laterals on the stem by
two-thirds of their
length; they are left in
place as "stem builders"

Prune sideshoots on
lower branches back
to 3–4 leaves

YEAR 2, SUMMER

Year 2, until all tiers are formed, summer
*An espalier establishes gradually, and the lowest
tiers fruit before the topmost tiers are formed.
As each tier is created, those below are summer-
pruned (above) to produce fruiting spurs
when the basal third of the sideshoots is ripe.*

Established espalier, summer
*Regular summer pruning is vital (below),
otherwise the main stem directs energy into
strong upper growth at the expense of lower
tiers. As spur systems become more complex,
thin them as shown on p.123, in winter.*

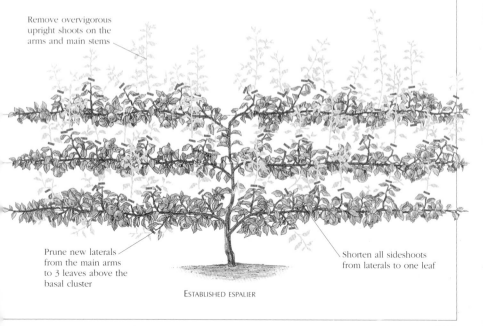

Remove overvigorous
upright shoots on the
arms and main stems

Prune new laterals
from the main arms
to 3 leaves above the
basal cluster

Shorten all sideshoots
from laterals to one leaf

ESTABLISHED ESPALIER

PEAR DWARF PYRAMID

THE DWARF PYRAMID is ideally suited to the pear's spur-bearing habit and can also be used for spur-bearing apples. Only 6ft (2m) is needed between trees, so it is a perfect form for small gardens, but if the trees are planted closely, precise training and regular summer pruning are essential to maintain the compact size and shape.

PRUNING AND TRAINING

Formative pruning and training concentrates on overcoming the naturally upright habit to reduce vigor and on forming an open branch structure, which radiates evenly around a strong central trunk. Begin with a young feathered tree with wide-angled laterals, and encourage this growth habit by cutting to outward-facing buds on the undersides of the shoots. Make your first priority the establishment of strong lower branches; vigorous shoots on the upper part of the stem must be removed. The pyramidal shape should admit sun and air to all parts of the plant without any overshadowing.

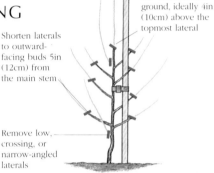

Cut the main stem to a bud 20–30in (50–75cm) above ground, ideally 4in (10cm) above the topmost lateral

Shorten laterals to outward-facing buds 5in (12cm) from the main stem

Remove low, crossing, or narrow-angled laterals

Year 1, winter
Dwarf pyramids need permanent staking, so insert a sturdy 6ft (2m) post on planting that will support the tree at maturity.

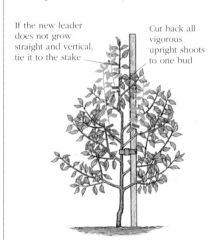

If the new leader does not grow straight and vertical, tie it to the stake

Cut back all vigorous upright shoots to one bud

Year 1, summer
Aim to maintain a strongly upright and vertical leading shoot and to reduce any upward-growing shoots from the laterals.

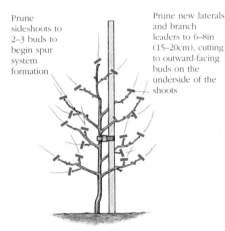

Prune sideshoots to 2–3 buds to begin spur system formation

Prune new laterals and branch leaders to 6–8in (15–20cm), cutting to outward-facing buds on the underside of the shoots

Year 2, winter
Cut the central leader to a bud, leaving 10in (25cm) of new growth. Choose one that faces the opposite way to the previous year's cut.

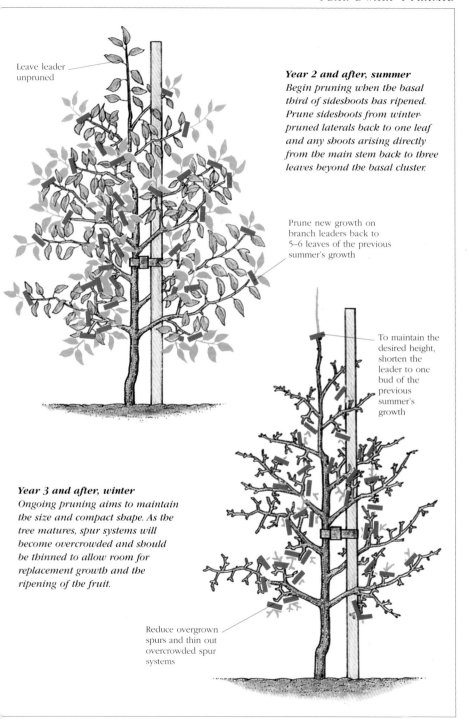

Leave leader unpruned

Year 2 and after, summer
Begin pruning when the basal third of sideshoots has ripened. Prune sideshoots from winter-pruned laterals back to one leaf and any shoots arising directly from the main stem back to three leaves beyond the basal cluster.

Prune new growth on branch leaders back to 5–6 leaves of the previous summer's growth

To maintain the desired height, shorten the leader to one bud of the previous summer's growth

Year 3 and after, winter
Ongoing pruning aims to maintain the size and compact shape. As the tree matures, spur systems will become overcrowded and should be thinned to allow room for replacement growth and the ripening of the fruit.

Reduce overgrown spurs and thin out overcrowded spur systems

Plum Pyramid

This form, when grafted onto the dwarfing rootstock 'Pixy', reaches no more than 6ft (2m) tall and, at spacings of 8–10ft (2.5–3m), is ideal for smaller gardens. A compact form that needs permanent staking, it suits all types of plums, including gages, damsons, and bullaces.

Pruning and training

Plums fruit at the base of one-year-old wood and along the length of two-year-old and older wood, so young growth is not routinely pruned as with apples and pears. All plums are susceptible to silver-leaf disease and cankers, so avoid winter pruning to reduce the risk of infection; delay any pruning that must be done during dormancy until early spring. Begin with a feathered tree, because all but the lowest laterals can be used for branch formation. Always make angled cuts to outward- or upward-facing buds whose direction of growth will reinforce the pyramidal outline.

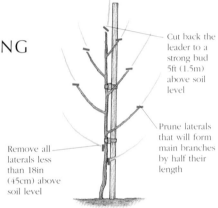

Cut back the leader to a strong bud 5ft (1.5m) above soil level

Prune laterals that will form main branches by half their length

Remove all laterals less than 18in (45cm) above soil level

Year 1, early spring
On trees with upright habits, cut laterals back to outward-facing buds; on spreading habits, cut to upward-facing buds. Check ties regularly.

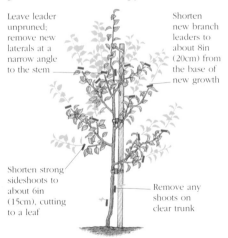

Leave leader unpruned; remove new laterals at a narrow angle to the stem

Shorten new branch leaders to about 8in (20cm) from the base of new growth

Shorten strong sideshoots to about 6in (15cm), cutting to a leaf

Remove any shoots on clear trunk

Year 1 until maturity, summer
Prune when the basal third of sideshoots is ripe. Continue to cut to upward- or outward-facing buds, as in early spring pruning.

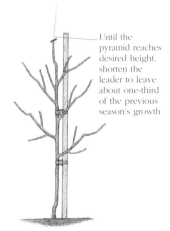

Until the pyramid reaches desired height, shorten the leader to leave about one-third of the previous season's growth

Year 2 until maturity, early spring
Keep spring pruning to a minimum. As the tree matures, delay shortening the leader until late spring to discourage regrowth.

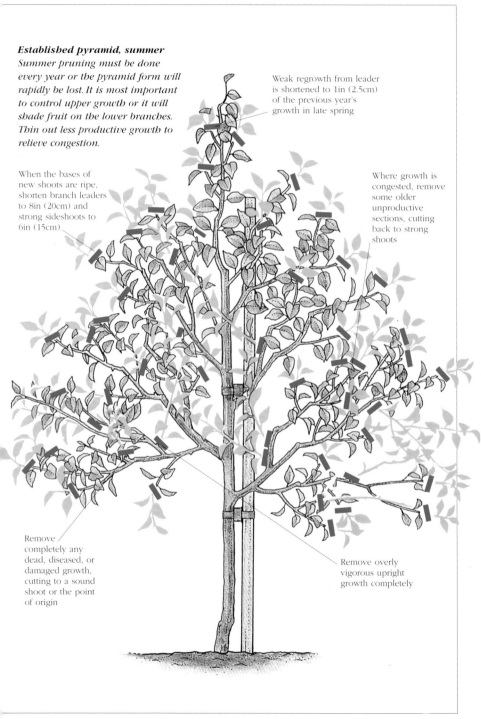

Established pyramid, summer
Summer pruning must be done every year or the pyramid form will rapidly be lost. It is most important to control upper growth or it will shade fruit on the lower branches. Thin out less productive growth to relieve congestion.

Weak regrowth from leader is shortened to 1in (2.5cm) of the previous year's growth in late spring

When the bases of new shoots are ripe, shorten branch leaders to 8in (20cm) and strong sideshoots to 6in (15cm)

Where growth is congested, remove some older unproductive sections, cutting back to strong shoots

Remove completely any dead, diseased, or damaged growth, cutting to a sound shoot or the point of origin

Remove overly vigorous upright growth completely

CHERRIES

SWEET AND DUKE CHERRIES fruit at the base of one-year-old and older wood. Two different cultivars are usually needed so cross pollination occurs. Since dwarfing rootstocks are not readily available, sweet and duke cherries are best for good-sized gardens. Select sour cherries for limited space: they are smaller, self-fertile, and fruit almost exclusively on the previous year's shoots.

SWEET OR DUKE CHERRY FAN

A fan trained against a sunny wall, on a system of horizontal wires, is ideal for sweet or duke cherries; the wall's warmth helps the fruit to ripen in cool-summer climates. Allow an area about 8ft (2.5m) in height by 15ft (5m) wide. As cherries are susceptible to silver-leaf disease, formative pruning takes place at bud-burst in spring. Start with a feathered whip, and plant in autumn to midwinter. In early spring, cut the leader back just above the topmost lateral. Select 2 to 4 strong laterals, and shorten to 16in

(40cm) from the main stem. Tie them to stakes attached at 45° angles to the wires. In midsummer, select and tie in shoots from sublaterals to form the ribs of the fan, aiming for even development on each side. Use well-placed sideshoots to fill the framework. Shorten surplus sideshoots to one leaf, and remove all growth below the lowest wires. To encourage branching, shorten the ribs in the early spring of the second and third years to leave 24–30in (60–75cm) of the previous year's growth.

Established fan, early summer
Prune to control growth in early summer and again after harvest. Remove young sideshoots that grow out from, or toward, the wall; thin the rest in spring to about 4in (10cm) apart.

In early summer, when they have 8–12 leaves, cut back laterals not needed to fill the framework to 6–7 leaves; pinch out regrowth and after harvest prune these laterals back to 3 leaves

Leave branch leaders alone until they fill allotted space

SOUR CHERRY BUSH

Although sour cherries are self-fertile, you still need 15ft (5m) of space for a bush form 12ft (4m) high. Start with a feathered whip. In early spring, cut the leader back to the top-most lateral, about 3ft (90cm) above ground. Shorten 3–4 well-spaced laterals by two-thirds to an outward-facing bud; these will form the main branch framework. Always cut to a pointed growth bud, rather than to a flower bud. Shorten low or narrow-angled laterals to two buds. Pinch out regrowth to two leaves during the summer. In the second spring, on each lateral, shorten 2–3 strong sideshoots by half to a bud that will produce a balanced crown. Remove badly placed shoots and low and previously shortened laterals. In the third spring, prune branch leaders by a quarter, to a bud that will grow to fill the framework.

Established bush
Prune partly in spring, partly after harvest. On older trees, in spring, when growth buds are clearly visible, cut back 1–2 branches or branch sections each year to encourage new growth, or delay until after harvesting when up to a quarter of the fruited shoots are cut back.

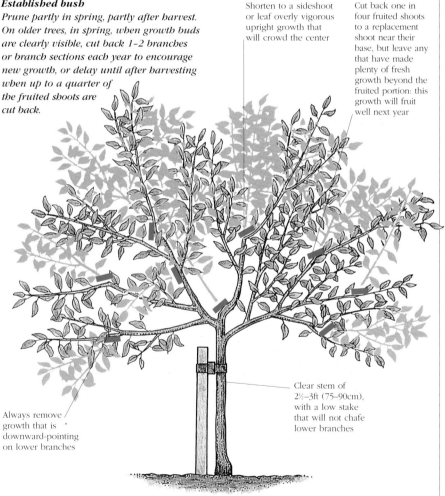

Shorten to a sideshoot or leaf overly vigorous upright growth that will crowd the center

Cut back one in four fruited shoots to a replacement shoot near their base, but leave any that have made plenty of fresh growth beyond the fruited portion: this growth will fruit well next year

Always remove growth that is downward-pointing on lower branches

Clear stem of 2½–3ft (75–90cm), with a low stake that will not chafe lower branches

FIGS

FIGS NEED LONG, HOT SUMMERS to fruit heavily. In warm countries, figs are grown as informal bush or half-standard trees. To bear well in cool climates, they need a warm, favored site and are pruned to be very open to let in light. The fan form is ideal for this, on a warm, sunny sheltered wall, but even there winter protection of netting filled with straw is advisable.

FRUITING HABIT

The fig has an unusual fruiting habit – figs at three stages of development are present all at once. First to ripen are overwintered embryo figs, produced in the leaf axils the previous year. Those formed in spring on new growth ripen next. In hot climates, they make up the main, late-summer crop; they seldom ripen well in cool-summer regions. Meanwhile, new embryos form in the upper leaf axils, to overwinter and ripen the following summer. In cool climates, pruning concentrates on encouraging embryo figs to form and giving them the best ripening conditions.

FRUITING DEVELOPMENT

On this unpruned shoot, a fig at the base that overwintered from last year is now ripening. Above it figs that form this spring will be next to ripen, if summer is long and hot. Embryo figs, forming in leaf axils at the tip, will ripen next year.

FIG FAN

A fig fan needs a space 7ft (2.1m) high by 12ft (4m) wide, and strong horizontal wires. Start with a 2–3-year-old plant with sturdy laterals. Build up a framework in the same way as for cherries (*see p.136*); aim to produce six main ribs on either side of a main stem over 2–3 winters; use laterals to fill out the framework. Prune figs in early spring, and in cool climates again in summer. In early spring, remove some older wood and cut a few young shoots back to one bud to boost new growth. Remove vigorous and overcrowded laterals.

Established fan, summer, cool climates
In summer, once the framework is complete, pinch back all new shoot tips to 5–6 leaves to stimulate new sideshoots.

FIG BUSH

Start with a two-year-old fig with 3–4 well-spaced laterals of equal vigor arising from the main stem at about 1½–3ft (45–90cm) above ground. A bush is ideal for containers, but here the trunk should be 16in (40cm) high to give stability. Plant and prune in late winter-early spring, or in cool climates when severe weather is over. Form a bush with 8–10 main branches arising at or near the trunk, as for an apple bush (*see p.126*). Prune established bushes in spring, and in cool climates again in summer, by pinching out new shoot tips when they have made 5–6 leaves. In cool climates, spring pruning keeps the bush as open and spreading as possible. In warm climates, the reverse is true. Cut spreading branches back to upright shoots and leave center growth to give protection from sun scorch.

Thin badly placed shoots and any that crowd the center of the bush

Cut bare or leggy shoots back to one bud, or 2–3in (5–8cm) to encourage new growth.

Established bush, spring, cool climates
First cut back any frost-damaged growth to healthy wood and aim to make all other cuts to maintain an open, spreading habit.

Pinch back new shoots to 5–6 leaves to encourage embryo fruits to form in the leaf axils

CITRUS FRUITS

MANY CITRUS TREES are grown for their ornamental value as well as for their fruit. In warm regions, they may crop for up to six months of the year in growth cycles of 4–6 weeks, and pruning may be done at any time. In cool climates, citrus trees must be protected from frost and cold. Prune young trees from spring to late summer, established trees at or after harvesting.

BRANCHED-HEAD STANDARD

In cooler climates, grow citrus trees under glass or in pots which can be transferred to a sheltered, sunny outdoor site during the summer. Citrus in containers look best as branched-head standards on a trunk of 3–5ft (1–1.5m). Feed young plants regularly each month during the growing season. Remove any shoots or suckers on the stem as soon as they develop. In spring, shorten any

shoots that have been cold-damaged. For well-established plants, reduce watering to a minimum for 3–4 weeks during early summer; this will promote flowering when watering resumes (citrus trees become dormant at temperatures below 55°F (13°C), or in drought conditions; the onset of rain or resumption of watering usually results in flowering within four weeks).

TRAINING A CITRUS STANDARD

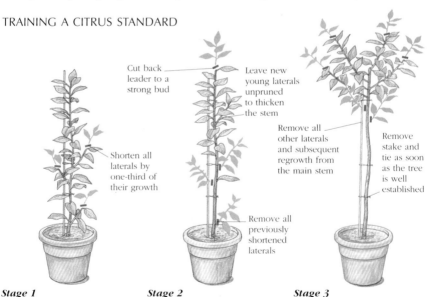

Cut back leader to a strong bud

Shorten all laterals by one-third of their growth

Leave new young laterals unpruned to thicken the stem

Remove all other laterals and subsequent regrowth from the main stem

Remove all previously shortened laterals

Remove stake and tie as soon as the tree is well established

Stage 1
A young, unbranched plant is lightly staked and the leader tied in to ensure vertical growth. Shorten all laterals by one-third of their length.

Stage 2
Once the desired height of the stem has been exceeded, prune the leader back to a strong bud. Remove the previously shortened laterals completely.

Stage 3
Select four well-spaced shoots from which to develop the head; tip-prune each by 3–4 leaves. Prune subsequently as for a bush tree (see opposite).

CITRUS BUSH

Cropping citrus trees are grown as bush trees on a trunk of at least 20in (50cm). The trunk is cleared gradually (*see p.34*), and once the desired height of clear trunk has been achieved, the crown is formed in much the same way as for a branched-head standard. Begin with a young unbranched plant; when it reaches 3–4ft (90–120cm) high, cut back the leader to 2ft (60cm). Select 3–4 strong laterals, at angles of at least 40° to the main stem, to form the branch framework. Shorten them in early spring to about 12in (30cm) from the main stem. In subsequent springs until established, shorten new branch leaders by one-third of their growth, and tip-prune sideshoots by 3–4 leaves.

Established bush, at or after harvesting
In general, prune mature trees as little as possible; remove dead or diseased wood regularly, and any crossing branches that could cause chafing damage.

Tip-prune branch leaders to maintain a balanced compact crown

Remove crossing and inward-growing shoots to create and maintain an open branch structure

On grafted trees, remove suckers that appear below the graft union; water shoots often appear on main branches, remove as seen

When harvesting, prune each fruited shoot back to a non-fruiting sideshoot as they will not fruit again; harvest with secateurs, keeping the calyx (whorl of sepals) intact to keep the fruit from rotting

SOFT FRUITS

THE TEXTURES and flavors of sun-warmed soft
fruits is a pleasure that even a small garden can
afford. You don't even need to grow them in a
traditional "model" fruit garden, for many are
equally at home in an ornamental garden,
especially when trained to restricted forms. Soft
fruits are generally cool-climate plants that enjoy
sun but dislike humidity and stagnant air. Most
are prone to viruses, but in the case of those that
are, new stock is usually available with virus-free
certification. Left unpruned, all soft fruits will
bear fruit after a fashion, but with correct pruning
and training you can establish a regular cycle of
renewal pruning, removing the old to make way
for the new, which guarantees healthy, fruitful
plants that bear luscious, flavorful crops of
the best possible quality and quantity.

Gooseberries *A bush fruit, the gooseberry is naturally shrubby and compact.*

BASIC TECHNIQUES

WITH THE EXCEPTION of autumn-fruiting raspberries, all woody soft fruits crop on stems that are at least a year old. This makes pruning fairly simple. On cane fruits and, to a lesser degree, blackcurrants, fruited wood is cut out after harvesting; on other bush fruits it is shortened, or "spurred back," annually to a semipermanent branch framework.

SOFT FRUIT FORMS

Cane fruits (raspberries, blackberries, and hybrids) produce new stems annually from the base, to replace fruited canes as they die. Pruning speeds up replacement, and training the new shoots makes harvesting easier. The more shrubby bush fruits, such as currants, gooseberries, and blueberries, fruit on sideshoots arising from one-year-old or older wood. Pruning aims to encourage the production of sideshoots and ensures regular replacement of fruiting wood.

Bush
Pruning and training aims to create a crown of well-spaced branches, to admit light and air to the center; a short stem or "leg" keeps fruits clear of the ground.
SUITABLE FOR *Red and white currants, gooseberries.*

Single cordon
An ideal form for spur-bearing fruits, giving high yields in restricted spaces. It is easy to net (all soft fruits attract birds), and is either grown singly or in rows trained on posts and wires.
SUITABLE FOR *Red and white currants, gooseberries.*

Multistemmed bush
The natural form of blackcurrants. They produce new shoots from the base each year to form an upright multistemmed bush. Pruning aims to ensure continued replacement of year-old wood, which is the most productive.

Canes: raspberry
Raspberries produce suckers freely, often at a distance from the original planting site. Pruning speeds production of new canes and, by selecting only well-placed replacements, aims to confine plants to bounds.

Canes: blackberry and hybrid berry
Canes develop from a more or less central point. They are separated and trained apart to receive light and air and to make harvesting from the thorny stems easy.

Routine tasks

There are two main pruning periods for soft fruits: winter and summer. Prune in winter to develop and improve a plant's shape, remove badly placed or old, unproductive growth in favor of young wood, reduce overcrowding, and open up the center of the bush. It should take place as late as possible in the season, so that any bird damage to buds can be taken into account when deciding what to cut out. Summer pruning is necessary only for trained forms,

to restrict growth and maintain the shape and structure. Soft fruits are particularly prone to serious viral diseases. Dig up and discard affected plants before starting to prune other plants. Remember that pruners and other tools can spread viruses, so disinfect thoroughly by dipping them in household disinfectant before and after pruning each plant. Aphids and other sap-sucking insects also spread virus diseases; look for and then control them immediately.

CANE FRUITS

Pruning cane fruits
Fruited canes are cut out with a straight cut across the stem at ground level, carefully avoiding young growth that is being retained.

Removing unwanted suckers
All canes begin as suckers from the roots or base of the plant. Hoe out any too far from the row, or remove (as above) *for propagation.*

BUSH FRUITS

Renewal pruning
With bush fruits (particularly blackcurrants) a proportion of older wood is taken out each winter to keep the center open and increase the proportion of the plant formed by one- and two-year-old shoots. The latter will fruit in the summer, while new shoots that will fruit the following year are developing. Cut fruited shoots back to the base or to a strong sideshoot lower down.

BLACKBERRIES

DESCENDED from woodland plants, the blackberry (*Rubus fruticosus*) and its cultivars, and hybrid berries – loganberries, tayberries, boysenberries, and katonahberries – (crosses between blackberries and other *Rubus* species) need a sunny site to produce crops of well-ripened fruit. All are cool climate fruits and are cultivated, trained, and pruned in the same way.

TRAINING METHODS

Blackberries and hybrid berries fruit on sideshoots arising from long, vigorous canes produced in the previous year. Pruning and training has several aims. Canes are trained to allow maximum exposure of the fruits to the ripening sun and to make harvesting easy; training also keeps fruits clean and clear of the ground and prevents stem tips from self-layering. They are pruned to encourage continuous production of vigorous healthy shoots, removing the old to make way for the new. These fruits are not certified to be virus-free, as raspberries are, so avoid buying any with mottled leaves or dwarfed growth.

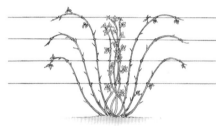

Fan (for less vigorous cultivars)
Fruiting canes are spread out and new canes tied in to the central space, to be lowered and tied into position once fruited canes have been cut away.

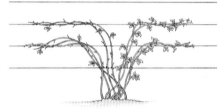

Alternate bay
Ideal where several plants grow along a wall. Train young and fruiting canes toward each other in the spaces between plants, or bays; the canes in each bay fruit in alternate years.

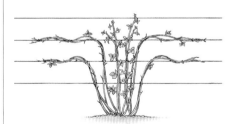

Rope (for cultivars with pliable stems)
Fruiting canes twisted into "ropes" are tied to the lower wires; new canes trained up the middle and along the top are allocated to the lower wires after fruited canes are cut out.

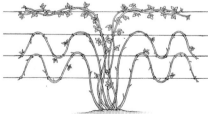

Weaving (for cultivars with pliable stems)
Fruiting canes are trained in a serpentine manner on lower wires; new ones are taken up the middle and along the top, to be lowered after fruited canes are cut out.

ESTABLISHED PRUNING

The aim is to maintain an annual succession of year-old, heavy-cropping canes. Once all berries have been harvested, cut out fruited canes and tie in new ones if required. If there are too few new canes to fill the space, retain a few old ones, cutting back their sideshoots to 1in (2.5cm). Remove any weak new canes and any that appear too far from the row. Canes may be bundled together for added winter protection and retrained in spring. At the end of winter, tip back canes by 6in (15cm).

FORMATIVE PRUNING

Plant one-year-old plants in early winter or, in severe climates, in early spring. Shorten the original cane to 8–12in (20–30cm) above ground on planting, to stimulate basal growth, then remove it completely in summer. New shoots, which are tied in as they develop, fruit in their second summer. Routine pruning takes place in autumn after harvesting, to remove all fruited canes and again in late winter or early spring, tipping back to encourage sideshoots and remove any frost-damaged growth.

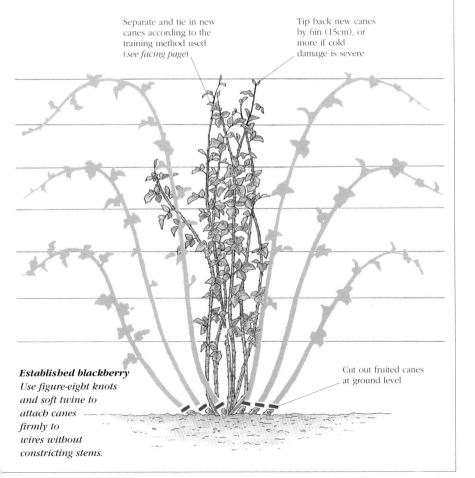

Separate and tie in new canes according to the training method used (*see facing page*)

Tip back new canes by 6in (15cm), or more if cold damage is severe

Established blackberry
Use figure-eight knots and soft twine to attach canes firmly to wires without constricting stems.

Cut out fruited canes at ground level

RASPBERRIES

NUMEROUS RASPBERRY CANES are produced directly from the mass of fibrous roots just below soil level. The canes of summer-fruiting raspberries grow one year and crop the next, after which they are removed at ground level. Autumn-fruiting raspberries produce canes that fruit at the end of a single season, from late summer to the first frosts, and are then cut to the ground.

TRAINING SYSTEMS

Open posts and wires systems are widely used for training. Good support is essential, especially for summer-fruiting cultivars, which must survive winter weather.

Scandinavian system

Suitable for less vigorous summer-fruiting cultivars, the Scandinavian system is ideal for a large, sheltered area where you want to grow a quantity of plants. With this training method, the canes are not tip-pruned. The canes are planted centrally, and 3–4 of the strongest from each plant are woven along wires and around each other. Tie in if necessary. New canes fill the central space, protected from wind and possible damage during harvesting. When the fruited canes are cut away, the replacement canes are woven into place.

Post-and-wire system

A compact, secure method, posts and wires are good for windy areas. The fruits receive maximum sun. Fruiting canes are tied in on one side of the wires; do not weave them in and out or they may chafe. New canes are loosely looped in around the wires.

VIRAL DISEASES

Raspberries are very prone to certain viral diseases for which there is no cure. Plants showing symptoms – short, weak canes, yellow-blotched foliage, and sparse, small or distorted fruits – must be dug up and discarded. Remove any suckers that grow from overlooked fragments. Do not replant raspberries for several years where virus-infected ones grew.

TRAINING METHODS

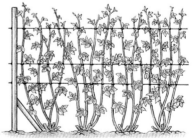

Scandinavian system
Drive 5ft (1.5m) posts 2ft (60cm)) into the ground, in two rows 3ft (90cm) apart, with posts set at 10ft (3m) intervals. Add diagonal support struts; run a single wire along each row.

Post-and-wire system
Stretch taut three wires at heights of 30in (75cm), 3ft (1m), and 5ft (1.5m) between two end posts or stapled along a line of 4–5 posts. Tie canes in on one side of the wire.

PLANTING AND PRUNING

Cultivation for summer- and autumn-fruiting raspberries is the same, except for pruning. Established summer-fruiting cultivars are pruned in late winter and after fruiting; autumn-fruiting raspberries in late winter.

Summer-fruiting raspberries

Plant as single canes, usually 24in (60cm) long, between late autumn and early spring. Shorten to 10in (25cm) on planting. Prune out the stumps in midsummer (*see right*). Tie in new canes as growth proceeds. Pinch out any flowers that appear, to conserve energy for next year's crop. Make sure the canes are well-supported over winter, tip-pruning them as winter ends (but not if using the Scandinavian system: *see opposite*). As soon as cropping has finished, cut fruited canes out at the base. Retain about eight strong new canes per plant, and tie in. Unless required as new plants, young canes emerging more than 8in (20cm) from the row should be removed by hoeing lightly.

Autumn-fruiting raspberries

These are bought as single canes and planted and pruned as for summer-fruiting cultivars. In summer the new canes will both grow and bear their first crop. As the canes grow, shorter cultivars such as 'September' will require no support, but more vigorous ones such as 'Autumn Bliss' need training to guard against wind damage. At winter's end, before any sign of growth, cut all canes to the ground. As the next year's young canes grow, remove weak and damaged growth. Do not tip-prune, since much of the fruit is borne at the top of the canes. Replace old plants when fruiting declines.

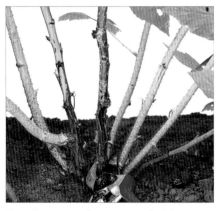

Year 1, summer for summer fruiting
The original cane of this summer-fruiting raspberry was shortened to 10in (25cm) on planting during the dormant season. Its stump is pruned out in midsummer.

ROUTINE TASKS, SUMMER-FRUITING RASPBERRIES

Fruited canes
Cut out at ground level, taking care not to damage current season's new shoots

Tying in new canes
Tie new canes 4in (10cm) apart, looping in with a continuous length of string.

Looping over
Bend very long canes over, tying to the top wire to avoid wind damage in winter.

Tip-pruning
At the end of winter, tip-prune canes by about 6in (15cm) to the same height.

CURRANTS

THE PRUNING of blackcurrants is very simple; all that is needed is the annual removal of older, less productive wood in favor of younger, more free-fruiting growth. Red- and whitecurrants fruit at the base of one-year-old laterals and are spur-pruned to a permanent framework of branches, with old wood taken out only in the event of disease, old age, or overcrowding.

BLACKCURRANT BUSH

Blackcurrants fruit most freely on shoots formed the previous summer, which are smooth and tea-colored. Some fruit is borne on the gray, shaggy two-year-old wood, but this is often worth sacrificing in favor of young growth. Begin with a certified virus-free two-year-old bush with 3–4 healthy shoots; it will bear in its second summer after planting. Plant when dormant, with the nursery soil mark about a thumb's width below ground. On vigorous, well-established bushes you can cut out entire fruited stems at harvest, tidying up what is left in winter. Aim for a balance of one- and two-year-old wood, retaining more of the latter on weak bushes to fill them out.

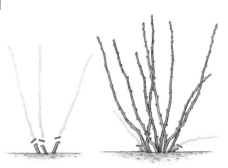

Years 1 and 2, winter
Immediately after planting, prune all shoots back hard to within one bud above soil level. In the second year, remove only weak or damaged shoots or those that are growing horizontally or downward.

Established bush
Prune at any time between cropping and late winter. Cut out all dark, three-year-old or older wood at the base

Retain strong two-year-old wood with plenty of new sideshoots

Remove less productive two-year-old wood with few sideshoots

Prune low, horizontal branches to a strong upward-growing shoot to restrict spread

Cut out older wood at the base

RED- AND WHITECURRANT CORDON

In winter red- and whitecurrants are hard-pruned to form spurs that fruit annually. These can be grown as an open-centered bush, as for gooseberries (*see pp.152–3*), and are also ideal trained as cordons. For this you will need a wall, fence, or pair of 6ft (2m) posts, fitted with horizontal wires at 12in (30cm) intervals. Begin with a one-year-old, single-stemmed currant. Plant it in winter, staking it with a cane tied to the wires. All cordons are pruned in summer and winter each year. In time, older spur systems will need thinning as for apples (*see p.123*). The leading shoot must be pruned back to a bud to restrict height once it reaches the top wire. Pinch out or shorten shoots that are growing toward the wall.

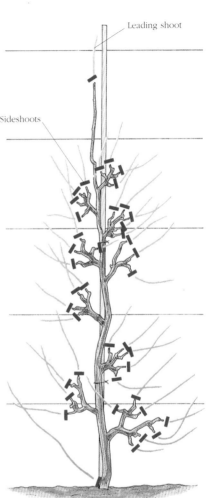

Leading shoot

Sideshoots

Pruning on planting
In winter, cut back the leading shoot by half its previous year's growth (left). *If a lower shoot is stronger, train this in instead. Cut back all other shoots to one bud.*

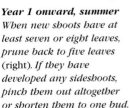

Year 1 onward, summer
When new shoots have at least seven or eight leaves, prune back to five leaves (right). *If they have developed any sideshoots, pinch them out altogether or shorten them to one bud.*

Year 2 onward, winter
Prune new growth on the leading shoot by a quarter each winter, cutting to a bud on the opposite side to last year's cut. When it reaches the top wire, prune new growth to one bud. Cut back all summer-pruned sideshoots, and any new ones, to one bud. Cut back to their point of origin any new shoots less than 4in (10cm) from the ground. Thin mature spurs when necessary.

GOOSEBERRIES

The growth habit of gooseberries varies between pendent and upright, depending on cultivar. Usually grown as a bush, gooseberries can be pruned in two ways: either on a loose renewal basis, or spur-pruned to a permanent framework. This option makes standard, fan, and cordon (*see p.151*) forms possible. Gooseberries fruit on year-old shoots and older spur systems.

GOOSEBERRY BUSH

The aim is to produce a bush 4–6ft (1.2–2m) tall with a strong framework of branches on a short leg. Start with a one-year-old plant with at least three strong shoots. Prune in late winter or just as buds burst in early spring; the later pruning reduces the impact of bird damage. In late winter after planting, shorten all shoots by about three-quarters; if this has already been done in the nursery, trim by ¾–1¼in (2–3cm). If the cultivar has a pendent habit, always cut to an upward-pointing bud. Sideshoots should develop during the next season, from which 8–10 are selected to form the main branches.

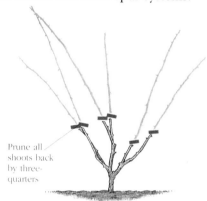

Prune all shoots back by three-quarters

Year 1, winter
In late winter, after planting, prune back each shoot by three-quarters to an outward-facing bud. On pendent cultivars, prune to an upward-facing bud.

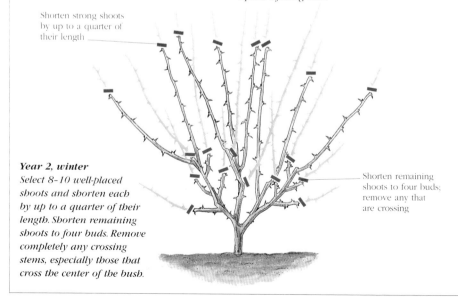

Shorten strong shoots by up to a quarter of their length

Year 2, winter
Select 8–10 well-placed shoots and shorten each by up to a quarter of their length. Shorten remaining shoots to four buds. Remove completely any crossing stems, especially those that cross the center of the bush.

Shorten remaining shoots to four buds; remove any that are crossing

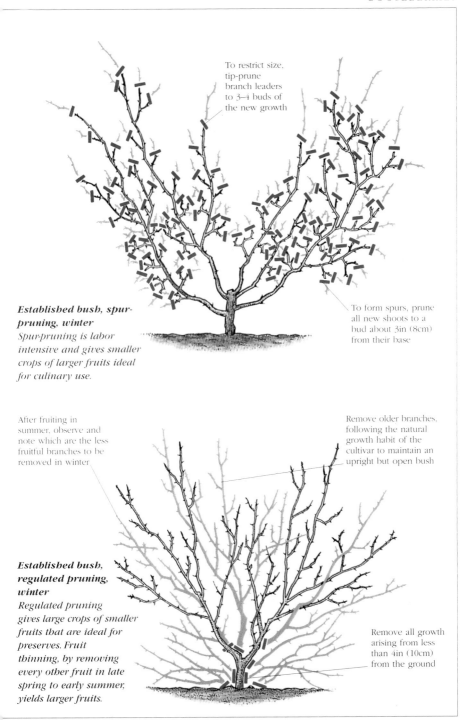

To restrict size, tip-prune branch leaders to 3–4 buds of the new growth

Established bush, spur-pruning, winter
Spur-pruning is labor intensive and gives smaller crops of larger fruits ideal for culinary use.

To form spurs, prune all new shoots to a bud about 3in (8cm) from their base

After fruiting in summer, observe and note which are the less fruitful branches to be removed in winter

Remove older branches, following the natural growth habit of the cultivar to maintain an upright but open bush

Established bush, regulated pruning, winter
Regulated pruning gives large crops of smaller fruits that are ideal for preserves. Fruit thinning, by removing every other fruit in late spring to early summer, yields larger fruits.

Remove all growth arising from less than 4in (10cm) from the ground

GLOSSARY

Adventitious bud Latent or dormant bud on a stem or root, often invisible until stimulated into growth.
Angle of attachment Angle at which a shoot develops from a main stem.
Apical bud A bud at the tip of a stem.
Apical dominance Controlling influence of the apical bud over the growth of a stem, which restricts development of lateral buds.
Axil The upper angle formed where a leaf stalk or sideshoot join the stem.
Axillary bud One that occurs in an axil.

Basal Growing at the base of a plant.
Basal cluster Lowest cluster of leaves on a shoot, at or around its point of origin.
Basal shoot A shoot arising from near or at ground level.
Bleeding The oozing of sap through a cut or wound.
Blind shoot A shoot that does not form a terminal flower bud, or one where the growing point has been destroyed.
Branch bark ridge A fold in bark where a branch joins the trunk, sometimes visible.
Branch collar A thickened ring of tissue at the base of a branch; a primary site of natural barriers.
Branch leader The leading shoot of a branch, where length is extended.
Break Used to describe new growth from a bud, such as the emergence of a shoot.
Bud A condensed shoot containing an embryonic leaf, leaf cluster, or flower.

Callus tissue Protective tissue formed by mainly woody plants to seal off a wound.
Cambium layer A layer of tissue beneath bark that produces new cells to increase the girth of stem and roots.
Coppicing Regular pruning back of trees or shrubs close to ground level to stimulate growth of vigorous shoots.
Crotch Angle between two branches, or between a branch and the trunk.

Crown Branched part of a tree above the trunk.
Crown lifting Removal of low branches to produce a taller clear trunk.
Crown reduction Making a crown smaller by cutting back the longest branches.
Crown thinning Removing crowded growth from the crown of a tree to admit more light.

Deadheading The removal of spent flowers or flowerheads.
Dieback Death of shoot tips that spreads down the stem, due to damage or disease.
Disbudding Removal of surplus buds to promote better quality fruits or flowers.
Dormancy State of temporary cessation of growth and slowing down of other life processes, usually during winter.
Dual leaders Competing leaders of equal strength.
Dwarfing rootstock In grafting, using roots of a smaller-growing plant than one grafted onto it to limit size of top growth.

Epicormic shoots Shoots that develop from adventitious buds, often at the site of pruning wounds.
Extension growth New growth made during the growing season.

Feathered whip One-year-old tree that has developed lateral shoots (feathers).
Framework Permanent branch structure of a tree or shrub.
Flower bud Bud from which a flower, followed by fruit, develops.

Graft union The point at which rootstock and scion are united.
Grafting Making an artificial union between the top-growth of one plant (scion) and the roots of another (rootstock) so that they function as one plant.

Internodal cut A cut made between two nodes or growth buds.

Latent bud A bud that fails to develop in the season it was formed, but remains dormant until stimulated into growth.

Lateral Side growth that arises from any root or shoot.

Lateral bud Bud that will form a sideshoot.

Leader A plant's main, usually central, stem.

Leading shoot The main central shoot of a plant, or of a main branch.

Maiden A tree in its first year (*See* feathered whip)

Maiden whip A tree in its first year, without lateral branches.

Natural barrier Internal chemical barrier produced by a plant to halt the spread of infection through the rest of the plant.

Occlusion Process by which a pruning cut or wound is sealed over with callus tissue.

Pinch pruning Method of pruning whereby shoot tips are removed with finger and thumb.

Pollarding Regular pruning back of main branches of a tree to the head of a main stem or trunk, or to a short branch framework (*cf.* coppicing).

Regulated pruning Occasional removal of sections of branches, or whole branches, from large woody plants to prevent congestion and stimulate younger growth.

Remedial pruning Removal of dead, diseased, and damaged wood to protect plant health.

Renewal pruning A system in which older growth is regularly removed in favor of younger growth.

Replacement shoot Strong young shoot left to grow where it will develop to replace old growth removed by pruning.

Rib Main branch of a fan-trained tree.

Ripe wood Mature, hardened wood.

Root-to-shoot ratio Proportional size of the root system to the top-growth.

Secondary growth Growth that appears after pruning in summer.

Self-fertile A plant that produces viable seed when fertilized with its own pollen.

Sideshoot A shoot growing out from a stem.

Silver-leaf A disease that attacks a wide range of shrubs and trees, especially *Prunus* and *Malus* (cherries, plums, apples), causing leaves to have a silvered or leaden appearance.

Soil mark The usually visible point on a plant's stem showing the original soil level before the plant was lifted in the nursery.

Sport Natural mutation of plant or part of a plant that differs from normal characteristics of habit, shape, size, form, or color.

Spur A short shoot or branchlet bearing flower buds, as on fruit trees.

Spur-bearing Bearing flowers and fruit on short shoots along the length of stems.

Stem builder Shoot on a main stem retained temporarily so that its leaves can nourish the main stem's vertical growth.

Stub Portion of stem remaining between the point where a cut is made and the next area of active growth below it.

Sublateral Sideshoot from a lateral shoot.

Target pruning Removing growth with as small a pruning cut as possible, so as not to breach a plant's natural barriers.

Terminal At the tip of a stem or branch.

Tip-bearing Carrying much of the fruit crop at or near the shoot tips.

Tip-pruning Pinching or cutting out shoot tips to encourage sideshoots to develop, or to remove damaged growth.

Tipping back *See* tip-pruning.

Truss Compact cluster of flowers or fruits. **V-angle** The crotch or angle between a branch and the main stem. **Vegetative growth** Nonflowering, usually leafy, growth.

Water shoots Sappy, fast-growing epicormic shoots, usually arising at the site of damage or pruning cuts.

Whip A single-stemmed young tree that has not yet developed lateral branches.

Wind rock The destabilization of a plant's roots by strong winds.

INDEX

Acknowledgments

Dorling Kindersley would like to thank Diana
Vowles and Lesley Malkin for editorial assistance;
Sonia Charbonnier for additional DTP design;
Angela Anderson for picture research; Alice Fairman
for overseas liaison; and Ella Skene for compiling
the index.

Photography credits

All photography by Peter Anderson, except for the
images on the pages specified below (b=below, l=left)

Eric Crichton Photos 14 bl, 19 bl
John Glover 116
John Finler 94
Andrew Lawson 54
National Trust Photographic Library:
  Neil Campbell-Sharp 2-3, 6
Derek St Romaine 72

Illustration

All artworks by Karen Cochrane, except for those
on pages 7, 27, 55, 73, 95, 117, and 143, which are
by Sarah Young

In addition to the above, the publishers would also like
to thank the staff of the Royal Horticultural Society
Publications.